Tea Cosies

Tea Cosies

Jenny Occleshaw

NEW
HOLLAND

First published in 2013 by New Holland Publishers Pty Ltd
London • Sydney • Cape Town • Auckland

Garfield House 86–88 Edgware Road London W2 2EA United Kingdom
1/66 Gibbes Street Chatswood NSW 2067 Australia
Wembley Square First Floor Solan Road Gardens Cape Town 8001 South Africa
218 Lake Road Northcote Auckland New Zealand

www.newhollandpublishers.com

A record of this book is held at the British Library or the National Library of Australia.

ISBN 9781742573472

Managing Director: Fiona Schultz
Publisher: Lliane Clarke
Designer: Tracy Loughlin
Editor: Simona Hill
Proofreader: Melanie Hibbert
Photographs: Graham Gillies
Production Director: Olga Dementiev
Printer: Toppan Leefung (China) Ltd
10 9 8 7 6 5 4 3 2 1

Keep up with New Holland Publishers on Facebook

www.facebook.com/NewHollandPublishers

Contents

Introduction

Welcome to a fascinating world of fun and frivolity. The humble tea cosy has undergone a delightful transformation and for little cost and a couple of evenings of knitting, you can make and customize a fabulous cosy for your teapot.

With the exception of a couple of patterns all the tea cosies featured are based on just two designs. The Circular Tea Cosy can be knitted in either double knitting (8-ply) wool or chunky (12-ply) yarn and is knitted, initially in the round, on a set of double-pointed needles. It features an attractive picot hem. Once you've knitted to the start of the handle and spout, the work is divided onto two needles and the back and front are knitted separately. The two halves are brought back together at the top of the handle so that a seamless top can be shaped.

The second design is the Blackberry-stitch Tea Cosy, which can also be knitted in double knitting (8-ply) wool or chunky (12-ply) yarn. This design is made in two pieces – a back and a front. Once the body of the cosy is knitted and stitched together, the spout and handle openings have little knitted hems to tidy the edges, though this design feature can also be customized, providing another opportunity to introduce texture and colour. Once your cosy body is finished you can have fun adding the embellishments.

Take your time when making small knitted items and, by all means, add your own ideas. When adding decorations I found it easier to work with the cosy on the pot. That way I had a firm surface on which to work and could turn the pot as I sewed.

I always use pure wool for my cosies as I love the feel of it as well as the colours, but you can vary the yarn, adding some mohair or textured yarn, if you like. Knit a sample square first to test how great the difference in size might be and calculate to make sure that your chosen yarn will fit the tea cosy.

Tea cosies make great gifts and I am sure anyone would be delighted to receive a one-of-a-kind handmade cosy.

Knitting Abbreviations
Beg: beginning
Cont: continue
Cm: centimetres
Dec: decrease
Inc: increase the number of stitches by knitting into the front and back of the next stitch
K: knit
M1: make 1 stitch by picking up the loop that lies between the two needles and knitting into the back

P: purl
Patt: pattern
Psso: pass slip stitch over
Rep: repeat
Sl: slip
St: stitch or stitches
St st: stocking stitch
Rem: remaining
Rep: repeat
Rs: right side
Tbl: through back of loops
Tog: together
Work x tog: knit or purl x stitches together

Ws: wrong side
Wyif: with yarn in front
Yfwd: yarn forward
Yrn: yarn round needle

Crochet Abbreviations
Ch: chain
Dbl: double
Dc: double crochet
Ss: slip stitch
Tr: treble
Dtr: double treble
Htr: half treble

Circular Tea Cosy

This tea cosy is great for knitters used to knitting on a set of four needles and is the basis for many of the projects in this book, such as Pomp and Circumstance and Under Green Willow. The tea cosy is cast onto three double-pointed knitting needles and then divides on to two sets of two needles for the sides. Once the knitting is sufficiently long enough to accommodate the spout and handle openings it switches back to three needles for the top shaping. Don't be put off if you haven't tried knitting on double-pointed needles before; it isn't difficult.

SIZE
To fit a 6-cup teapot

MATERIALS
2 x 50 g balls of DK (8-ply) wool
4 x 4 mm double-pointed
    knitting needles
Wool needle

Using 3 x 4 mm double-pointed knitting needles and dk (8-ply) yarn, cast on 90 sts (30, 30, 30). Join into a ring, being careful not to twist the stitches.

Work 5 rounds of st st (knit every round).

Picot round: *Yfwd, k2tog, rep from * to end of round.

Work another 5 rounds st st.

Round 12: Fold the hem at the picot round and knit 1 stitch together with 1 loop from the cast-on edge until all stitches have been worked. Work another 5 cm in st st.

Divide for Spout and Handle Openings

Next round: Place a stitch marker at the start of the round. Knit the first 45 sts on to 1 needle. (These will become the first side. Knit the remaining 45 sts onto another needle. Knit backwards and forwards, working in rows on the first 45 sts.) Turn.

Next row: K4, purl to last 4 sts, k4.

Next row: Knit.

Rep the last 2 rows until work measures 16 cm from beg. Break off yarn.

Rejoin yarn and work other side to match, keeping garter st border correct.

Redistribute the stitches evenly on 3 needles ready to commence top shaping. Ensure that round starts with stitch marker.

Shape Top

Round 1: *K7, k2tog, rep from * to end.

Round 2 and alt rounds: Knit.

Round 3: *K6, k2tog, rep from * to end.

Round 5: *K5, k2tog, rep from * to end.

Keeping pattern of decreases, continue in this manner until the round k1, k2tog has been worked. Break off yarn. Thread through rem sts, pull up tight and fasten off.

To Make Up Cosy Darn in all loose ends.

Blackberry-stitch Tea Cosy

This blackberry-stitch tea cosy is knitted in two pieces and is the basis for many of the tea cosies in this book. It can be knitted in either double knit (8-ply) or chunky (12-ply) yarn, although the chunky version will knit up a little larger. The handle and spout sections are finished with a knitted hem, which is made by picking up stitches along the sides of the cosy and knitting an additional number of rows. The hem can be a contrast colour for visual impact. Always use good-quality yarn so your teapot stays warm.

SIZE
To fit a 6-cup teapot

MATERIALS
2 x 50 g balls of chunky (12-ply)
    or DK (8-ply) wool
1 pair 4 mm knitting needles
Wool needle

Note DK (8-ply) size is given in brackets.

Using 4 mm knitting needles, cast on 46 (54) sts.
Commencing with a knit row, work 6 (8) rows
st st.
Picot row: K1, *yfwd, k2tog, rep from * to last
2 sts, k2.
Commencing with a purl row, work another
7 (9) rows st st.
Next row: Wth rs facing, fold up hem at picot
edge and knit 1 st together with 1 loop from
cast-on edge until all sts have been worked.

Commence Pattern
Row 1: Knit.
Rows 2, 4 and 6: Purl.
Row 3: P1, *k, p, k all into same st, p3tog, rep
from * to last st, p1.
Row 5: P1, *p3tog, k, p, k all into same st, rep
from * to last st, p1.
These 6 rows form pattern.
Continue in pattern until work measures 17 cm
from picot edge ending with row 6.

Top Shaping
Next row: P1, *p1, p3tog, rep from * to end.
Next row: K2tog all across.
Break off yarn, thread through rem sts. Pull up
tightly and fasten off.
Make 2.

To Make Up Cosy With right sides together and
working out from the centre point down, stitch
the top seam closed for 5–6 cm on each side.
Turn right side out.

Handle and Spout Openings
Using 4 mm needles and with rs facing, pick
up and knit 48 (55) sts along both sides of both
pieces.
Work 12 rows st st. Cast off.

To Make Up Handle and Spout Hems Fold
the hem piece in half to the wrong side and stitch
in place.
Join the bottom seam for approximately 3–4 cm.
Sew in all loose ends.

Abstract Art

A tea cosy is a great canvas for some knitted modern art. These abstract dimensional shapes are knitted in bright colours, creating a dramatic contrast with the dark background. Reminiscent of children's drawings of spaceships, the dimensional shapes are great fun to knit. The cosy is topped with a knitted I-cord made using the same colours as the abstract shapes.

SIZE
To fit a 6-cup teapot

MATERIALS
4 x 50 g balls DK (8-ply) dark grey wool
Oddments of bright pink, bright green and oatmeal DK (8-ply) wool
1 pair 4.5 mm knitting needles
1 pair 3 mm knitting needles
2 x 4 mm double-pointed knitting needles
Polyester fibre filling
Wool needle

Using 4.5 mm knitting needles and 2 strands of dark grey, cast on 46 sts.

Row 1: K1, p1, *k2, p2, rep from * to last 2 sts, p1, k1.

Row 2: *K2, p2, rep from * to end.

These 2 rows form rib pattern.

Continue in rib until work measures 17 cm from beg.

Shape Top

Row 1: K1, p1 *k2, p2tog, rep from * to last 4 sts, k2, p1, k1.

Row 2: K2, *p2, k1 rep from * to last 4 sts, p2, k2.

Row 3: K1, p1, *k2tog, p1, rep from * to last st, k1.

Row 4: K2, p1, *k1, p1, rep from * to last 2 sts, k2.

Row 5: *Sl1, k1, psso, rep from * to last st, k1.

Row 6: K1, purl to last st, k1.

Row 7: K1, k2tog to last st, k1 (7 sts).

Row 8: As row 6.

Row 9: K1, k2tog 3 times.

Break off yarn, thread through rem sts, pull up tightly and fasten off.

Make 2.

To Make Up The Cosy With right sides together, stitch the top closed for approximately 5 cm down each side. Stitch up from the lower edge for 4 cm, leaving an opening for the handle and the spout. Turn right side out.

I-CORD LOOP TOP DECORATION

Using 4 mm double-pointed knitting needles and 2 strands of yarn, cast on 3 sts, knit 1 row, do not turn, *slide sts to other end of needle and pull yarn firmly behind, knit next row. Repeat from * until cord is 10 cm long. Slip first st, k2tog, psso,

fasten off.

Fold the I-cord in half to create a loop. Using one of the cast-on or cast-off yarn ends, stitch the I-cord into a loop, then sew the loop to the top of the cosy. Make 6 in your choice of colour and sew to the top of the cosy.

SMALL CIRCLES

Using 3 mm knitting needles and DK (8 ply), cast on 45 sts.

Commencing with a purl row, st st 4 rows.

Row 5: Knit.

Row 6: Knit.

Row 7 and all odd rows: Purl.

Row 8: *K3, k2tog, rep from * to end.

Row 10: *K2, k2tog, rep from * to end.

Row 12: *K1, k2tog, rep from * to end.

Row 14: K2tog all across.

Break off yarn, thread through rem sts, pull up tightly and fasten off.

Make 4 in contrasting colours.

To Make Up The Small Circles Press lightly, then oversew the row ends together. Turn the edge inwards so that it lies flat.

Place 2 small circles together, folding the hems inwards and stitching closed all around the outer edge. Repeat with the remaining pair.

TWISTED CORDS

Using 3.25 mm knitting needles, cast on 25 sts.

Inc in every st (50 sts).

Knit 1 row, Cast off purlwise. Make 2.

Attach to the centre of the small circles.

LARGE CIRCLES

Using 3 mm knitting needles and DK (8 ply), cast on 36 sts.

Purl 1 row.

Row 2: *K1, inc in next st, rep from * to end (54 sts).

Commencing with a purl row, work 3 rows st st.

Work 2 rows st st, beg with a purl row.

Beg with a knit row, work 2 rows st st.

Row 10: *K4, k2tog, rep from * to end.

Purl all odd rows.

Row 12: *K3, k2tog, rep from * to end.

Row 14: *K2, k2tog, rep from * to end.

Row 16: *K1, k2tog, rep from * to end.

Row 18: K2tog all across.

Break off yarn, thread through rem sts, pull up tightly and fasten off.

Make 4 in contrasting colours.

To Make Up The Large Circles Press lightly, then oversew the row ends together. Turn the edge inwards so that it lies flat. Place 2 large circles together and stitch closed all around the outside edge. Repeat with the remaining pair of large circles.

CONE

Using 3 mm knitting needles and DK (8 ply), cast on 20 sts.

Purl 1 row.

Row 2: *K1, inc in next st, rep from * to end (40 sts).

Commencing with a purl row, work 3 rows st st.

Work 2 rows st st, beg with a purl row.

Beg with a knit row, work 2 rows st st.

Row 10: *K4, k2tog, rep from * to end.

Purl all alternate rows.

Row 12: *K3, k2tog, rep from * to end.

Row 14: *K2, k2tog, rep from * to end.

Row 16: *K1, k2tog, rep from * to end.

Row 18: K2tog all across.

Break off yarn, thread through rem sts, pull up tightly and fasten off.

Make 2.

To Make Up The Cone Join row ends together and turn in hem at garter st edge. Stuff cones firmly with polyester fibre filling and sew to the centre of the large circle with small sts around the outer edge.

Adding The Decorations Attach one small circle and one large circle to each side of the cosy. Stitch firmly through the centre of the shape other wise you will spoil the shape of the ribbed pattern and prevent the cosy from being elastic.

Blue Moves

Unlike other tea cosies, this design fully encloses the teapot rather than sitting over it. The knitted sides and base are made as a continuous piece and the result, particularly when knitted in chunky wool, is to keep the pot really hot. At the top a row of eyelets, complete with drawstring I-cord or ribbon, completes the cosy, ensuring the fabric can be drawn together to create a snug fit.

SIZE
To fit a 6-cup teapot

MATERIALS
2 x 50 g balls chunky (12-ply) wool
Small amount mohair DK (8 ply) in second colour
1 m ribbon (optional)
4 x 4 mm double-pointed knitting needles
4 x 2.75 mm double-pointed knitting needles

BASE

Using 3 of the 4 mm double-pointed knitting needles, cast on 8 sts (2, 3, 3).

Join into a ring, being careful not to twist the sts.

Round 1: Knit.

Round 2: *M1, k1, rep from * to end.

Round 3: Knit.

Round 4: *M1, k2, rep from * to end.

Round 5: Knit.

Round 6: * M1, k3, rep from * to end.

Round 7: Knit.

Round 8: *M1, k4, rep from * to end.

Round 9: Knit.

Round 10: *M1, k5, rep from * to end.

Round 11: Knit.

Round 12: *M1, k6, rep from * to end.

Round 13: Knit.

Round 14: *M1, k7, rep from * to end (64 sts).

Set aside. Make another base adding 1 additional round of knit sts after row 14.

Place the 2 pieces on the needles right sides together with the smaller base in front. Insert the tip of a third needle through the first stitch in the smaller base, then through the first stitch in the outer base and knit the 2 sts tog. Continue until all sts have been worked in this way and the bases are joined together.

SIDES

Next round: *M1, k8, rep from * to end.

Next round: Knit.

Next round: *M1, k9, rep from * to end (80 sts).

Next round: Knit.

Next round: *M1, k10, rep from * to end (88 sts).

Next round: K44 and leave these sts on spare needles. Work first side on rem 44 sts.

Work backwards and forwards in rows as follows:

Next row: K4, purl to last 4 sts, k4.

Next row: Knit.

Rep these 2 rows until work measures 12 cm from base. Change to k2, p2 rib.

Work in rib for another 5 cm.

Eyelet row: K1, *yfwd, k2tog, rep from * to last st, k1.

Cont in k2, p2 rib for another another 5 cm.

Cast off.

Rejoin yarn to remaining sts and complete to match first side.

I-CORD FASTENER

Using 2.75 mm double-pointed knitting needles and blue or contrasting DK (8-ply) yarn, cast on 3 sts. Make an I-cord at least 40 cm long or to the desired length. Keep in mind that you need to lift the teapot out easily and you won't be able to do this if the I-cord is too short.

Thread the I-cord through the eyelet holes, pull up and tie in a bow. Alternatively, use ribbon.

LEAVES

Using 2.75 mm double-pointed knitting needles and DK (8-ply) mohair, cast on 3 sts. Work an I-cord for 1.5 cm to form the stem. Continue as follows:

Row 1: Knit.

Row 2: Purl.

Row 3: K1, m1, k1, m1, k1.

Row 4 and all even rows: Knit first and last st, and purl rem sts.

Row 5: K2, m1, k1, m1, k2.

Row 7: K3, m1, k1, m1, k3.

Row 9: K4, m1, k1, m1, k4.

Row 11: K5, m1, k1, m1, k5.

Rows 13 and 15: Knit.

Row 17: K5, sl2, k1, psso, k5.

Row 19: K4, sl2, k1, psso, k4.

Row 21: K3, sl2, k1, psso, k3.

Row 23: K2, sl2, k1, psso, k2.

Rows 24 and 26: Purl.

Row 25: K1, sl2, k1, psso, k1 (3 sts).

Row 27: K1, sl2, psso, fasten off.

Make at least 3.

To Add The Decorations Pin the leaves at random to the body of the tea cosy. Once you are happy with the arrangement, stitch securely in place.

Chickens in the Garden

This tea cosy was inspired by the three little pet chickens who live in my grandson's garden. I have designed them so that they huddle together at the top of the cosy in among some green foliage and surrounded by brightly coloured daisies. Make sure you stuff the chickens really firmly so that they are plump and stand upright. I used Regia Hand-Dye Effect sock yarn, and the effect, once knitted, gives each chicken a slightly different colour. Any 4-ply yarn in shades of brown would work well.

SIZE
To fit a 6-cup teapot

MATERIALS
4 mm knitting needles
1 pair of 2 mm knitting needles
1 pair of 2.75 mm double-
    pointed knitting needles
1 x 50 g ball oatmeal DK
    (8-ply) or chunky (12-ply)
    wool
2 x 50 g balls of sage green
    DK (8-ply) or chunky
    (12-ply) wool
Small amount of bright green
    DK (8 ply) wool for the leaves
Wool needle
Small amount of brown Regia
    Hand-Dye Effect 4-ply sock
    yarn for the chickens
Small amount of 4-ply yarn
    in cream, orange, pink, red,
    and yellow for the flowers
    and details
3 mm crochet hook
Polyester fibre filling

Using a pair of 4 mm knitting needles and the oatmeal yarn, cast on 46 sts (12-ply) or 54 sts (8-ply).

Beginning with a knit row, work 6 (8) rows st st.

Picot edge row: K1, *yfwd, k2tog, rep from * to last 2 sts, k2.

Beginning with a purl row, work another 7 (9) rows st st.

Next row: With right side facing, fold up hem at picot edge and knit 1 st together with loop from cast-on edge until all sts have been worked.

Change to sage green yarn and commence pattern as follows:

Row 1: Knit.

Rows 2, 4 and 6: Purl.

Row 3: P1, *k, p, k into same st, p3tog, rep from * to last st, p1.

Row 5: P1, *p3tog, k, p, k into same st, rep from * to last st, p1.

These 6 rows form pattern.

Continue in patt until work measures 17 cm from picot edge row, ending with a row 6.

Decrease row: P1, *p1, p3tog, rep from * to end.

Next row: K2tog all across.

Break off yarn, and thread through rem sts. Pull up tightly and fasten off. Make 2.

To Make Up The Cosy With right sides together, starting from the centre, stitch the top seam closed for 5–6 cm down each side. Turn right side out.

Handle and Spout Openings

Using 4 mm needles and oatmeal chunky (12-ply) or DK (8-ply) wool, and with the right side facing, pick up and knit 48 (55) sts along the spout and handle edge of each side of the tea cosy. Work 12 rows st st. Cast off.

Fold each oatmeal piece in half to the wrong side and carefully stitch in place. Sew the tea cosy together at each bottom side edge for 3–4 cm. Sew in any loose ends.

I-CORD LEAVES

Using 2.75 mm double-pointed knitting needles and bright green DK (8 ply), cast on 3 sts. Work an I-cord for 1.5 cm for the stem following the instructions in the introduction. Continue:

Next row: Knit.

Row 2: Knit.

Row 3: K1, m1, k1, m1, k1.

Row 4 and all even rows: Knit.

Row 5: K2, m1, k1, m1, k2.

Row 7: K3 m1, k1, m1, k3.

Row 9: K4, m1, k1, m1, k4.

Row 11: K5, m1, k1, m1, k5.

Rows 13 and 15: Knit.

Row 17: K5, sl2, k1, psso, k5.

Row 19: K4, sl2, k1, psso, k4.

Row 21: K3, sl2, k1, psso, k3.

Row 23: K2, sl2, k1, psso, k2.

Rows 24 and 26: Purl.

Row 25: K1, sl2, k1, psso, k1 (3 sts).

Row 27: K1, sl2, psso, fasten off.

Make 5.

To Complete The Leaves Sew the leaves around the top of the tea cosy with the stalks to the centremost point.

CHICKENS

Using 2 mm knitting needles and Regia Hand-Dye Effect 4-ply yarn, cast on 25 sts.
Row 1: Purl.
Row 2: K1, m1, k9, k2tog, k1, sl1, k1, psso, k9, m1, k1 (25 sts).
Row 3: Purl.
Repeat rows 2 and 3 twice more.
Row 8: K1, m1, k23, m1, k1.
Commencing with a purl row, work 5 rows st st.
Row 14: K12, m1, k3, m1, k12.
Row 15: Purl.
Row 16: K13, m1, k3, m1, k13.
Row 17: Purl.
Row 18: K1, sl1, psso (5 times), k4, m1, k3, m1, k4, k2tog (5 times).
Row 19: Purl.
Row 20: (Sl1, k1, psso) 3 times, k4, m1, k3, m1, k4, k2tog (3 times) (19 sts).
Row 21: Cast off 4 sts, purl to end.
Row 22: Cast off 4 sts, k3, m1, k3, m1, k4.
Row 23: Purl.
Row 24: Knit.
Row 25: P1,*p2tog, rep from * to end.
Break off yarn, thread through rem sts, pull up tightly and fasten off.
Make 3.

To Make Up The Chickens The garter st side is the right side. Sew up the centre seam to form the tummy, stuffing the body firmly as you go. The tip of a pen can be handy to ensure the beak is firm.

Wings

Using 2 mm knitting needles and Regia Hand-Dye Effect 4-ply, cast on 11 sts. Working in garter st, knit 3 rows.
Begin wing shaping: K1, sl1, k1, psso, knit to end. Repeat this row until 3 sts rem.
Break off yarn, thread through rem sts, pull up tightly and fasten off. Make 6.
Fold each wing in half and stitch closed. Place one wing on each side of each chicken with the wide end towards the rear. Stitch in place.

Beak and Crest

Using yellow 4-ply, embroider the beak using straight stitches.
To make the red crest, using red 4-ply make a straight stitch on top of the head, but not too tight. Make a few stitches around this straight stitch to give a curly effect.
Attach each chicken securely to the top of the cosy, making them all face in towards each other.

FLOWERS

Using a 3 mm crochet hook and 4-ply yarn make 6ch and form into a loop with a sl st. Break off yarn and join in second colour. Work 1ch, then 11dc into the loop formed. Sl st into first dc. Make *11ch, sl st into next dc, rep from * until 12 petals have been completed. Fasten off.
Make at least 6 flowers using different combinations of colours. Adjust the size of the flowers, if you like ,by reducing the number of chains used in the petals.
Position the daises when the tea cosy is on the teapot. Pin each in place, then stitch securely.

Christmas Snowballs

This is a fabulously ostentatious tea cosy that would make a perfect Christmas gift for a tea drinker. Knitting in stocking stitch in soft cream yarn, this cosy is adorned with more than 40 fun crocheted snowballs and topped with a lavish knitted and decorated Christmas wreath.

SIZE
To fit a 6-cup teapot

MATERIALS
4 x 50 g balls of white or cream DK (8-ply) wool
4 x 4 mm double-pointed knitting needles
Wool needle
25 g green 4-ply
1 pair 2 mm knitting needles
Polyester fibre filling
50 cm narrow red and white ribbon
Red 8 mm Swarovski crystal beads
Beading needle
Red polyester thread
1 pair 2.75 mm double-pointed knitting needles
Polyester fibre filling

Using three 4 mm double-pointed knitting needles and cream or white DK (8-ply) yarn, cast on 90 sts, (30, 30, 30).

Join into a ring, being careful not to twist the stitches.
Work 5 rounds st st (every round knit).
Picot edge: *Yfwd, k2tog, rep from * to end of round.
Work another 5 rounds st st.
Round 12: Fold hem at picot edge and knit 1 stitch together with 1 loop from cast-on edge until all stitches have been worked.
Work another 5 cm in st st.

Divide for Spout and Handle Openings
Place stitch marker. K45 sts on to one needle. You will now be knitting backwards and forwards in rows on the first 45 sts. Turn.
Row 2: K4, purl to last 4 sts, k4.
Row 3: Knit.
Rep the last 2 rows until work measures 16 cm from beg. Break off yarn.
Rejoin yarn and work other side to match, keeping garter stitch border correct.
Redistribute stitches evenly on to three needles, ensuring that round starts in line with the stitch marker.

Shape Top
Round 1: *K7, k2 tog, rep from * to end.
Round 2 and all even rounds: Knit.
Round 3: *K6, k2tog, rep from * to end.
Round 5: *K5, k2tog, rep from * to end.
Keeping pattern of decreases, continue in this manner until the round k1, k2tog has been worked. Break off yarn. Thread through rem sts, pull up tight and fasten off.

SNOWBALLS
Using 2.75 mm knitting needles and cream or white DK (8-ply) yarn, cast on 12 sts.
Row 1: Knit.
Row 2: P10, wrap.
Row 3: K8, wrap.
Row 4: P6, wrap.
Row 5: K4, wrap.
Row 6: Purl.
Rep these 6 rows another 4 times. Cast off. With right sides together sew side seam half way. Turn right side out and stuff firmly. Sew the rest of the seam and then run a gathering thread around the cast-on edge. Pull up firmly and fasten off. Do the same with the other end. Make at least 40 balls.

Starting at the lower edge, sew the snowballs firmly to the cosy. It is easier to do this with the cosy on the teapot.

CHRISTMAS WREATH
Using 2 mm knitting needles and dark green 4-ply yarn, cast on 14 sts. Knit 1 row.
Row 2: Knit.
Row 3: K10, turn.
Row 4: Knit to end.
Row 5: Knit to end.
Repeat rows 2–5 another 20 times.
Knit 1 row. Cast off. Sew row ends together. Stuff firmly to make a circle.

To Decorate Sew one end of the ribbon in place under the wreath and then wind diagonally around the wreath. Using a beading needle and red cotton, sew the beads on to the wreath at random intervals and then attach the wreath securely to the top of the tea cosy

Curious Curves

This unusual curvy tea cosy is constructed of knitted scallops, made in a similar way to a traditional mitred square. Six scallops are knitted together to make four quarters of the cosy, which are then sewn together. The top knot and the side scallops are stuffed with lightweight fibre filling to help the cosy hold its shape. The whole cosy slots over the teapot with no allowance for a large spout or handle.

SIZE
To fit a 6-cup teapot

MATERIALS
1 x 50 g ball aqua DK (8-ply) wool
1 x 50 g ball multi-coloured blue DK (8-ply) wool
1 x 50 g ball bright blue DK (8-ply) wool
1 x 50 g ball light blue DK (8-ply) wool
1 pair 4 mm knitting needles
1 pair 3.25 mm knitting needles
Wool needle
Polyester fibre filling

The tea cosy is made up of four panels, each containing six curved shapes (24 in total).
The curved shapes are each knitted in two contrasting colours using the aqua and different shades of blue wool.

CURVED SHAPES

Using 4 mm knitting needles and DK (8-ply), cast on 33 sts using colour A.

Row 1: Knit first stitch tbl, k to last st, sl last st purl wise wyif.

Rows 2 and 3: Knit using colour B.

Row 4: Using colour A, k1 tbl, *sl1, k1, repeat from * to last st, sl1 purlwise wyif.

Row 5: Using colour A, k1, *sl1 wyif, k1, repeat from * to last st, sl1 purlwise wyif.

Rows 6 and 7: As rows 2 and 3.

Row 8: As row 4.

Row 9: As row 5.

Row 10: Using colour B, k1 tbl, k to last st, sl1 purlwise wyif.

Row 11: Using colour B, k2tog all across row to last st, sl1 purlwise wyif.

Row 12 As row 4.

Row 13: As row 5.

Row 14: Using colour B, k1 tbl, knit to last st, sl1 purlwise wyif.

Row 15: K2togtbl, *K1, k2tog, rep from * to last 2 sts, k1, sl1 purlwise wyif.

Remaining rows are worked in moss stitch.

Row 16: K2tog tbl, moss st to last st, sl1 purlwise wyif.

Rows 17–22: K1 tbl, moss st to last st, sl1 purlwise wyif.

Rows 23–31: K2tog tbl at beg of each row, until 3 sts rem, k3tog tbl. Break off yarn, pull through rem st and fasten off.

Joining Curved Shapes Place the points of two curved edges right sides together. With 4 mm knitting needles, pick up and knit 17 sts along the curved edge of first shape and then 16 sts from second shape (33 sts).

To Make Up The Cosy To make each quarter section you need three shapes along the bottom row, two in the second row and one on the top. This gives a pyramid shape with a scalloped edge. Two quarters are joined together along a straight edge to make one side of the cosy. Make 2.

With right sides together, sew the front and back cosy together beginning at the point between the first and second scallop on the bottom row and working around the scallops to finish with the scallop at the opposite side. Turn right side out.

Using 3.25 mm knitting needles and one of the shades of blue DK (8-ply) yarn, pick up and knit 105 sts around the base, leaving the stitched up scallops clear.

Begin with a purl row, work 5 rows st st. Change to contrast blue and work 2 rows. Return to the original colour and work another 5 rows st st. Cast off. Fold half of hem to inside and slip st in place.

Stuff the two end shells firmly with polyester fibre filling and stitch closed.

Stuff the topmost shell in the same way.

Crazy Echidna

This loopy stitch tea cosy makes an unusual statement piece. Take time to learn this stitch, practising it first on some oddments of wool until you achieve a uniform tension. The finished effect is fantastic and the cosy is so thick it will keep your tea hot for a long time. If you are not a fan of the muted colours, it would look just as good in bright tones.

SIZE
To fit a 6-cup teapot

MATERIALS
2 x 50 g balls dark grey DK (8-ply) wool
2 x 50 g balls chocolate DK (8-ply) wool
2 x 50 g balls rust DK (8-ply) wool
2 x 50 g balls beige DK (8-ply) wool
2 x 50 g balls cream DK (8-ply) wool
1 pair 4.5mm knitting needles
4 x 2.75mm double-pointed knitting needles
Wool needle
Polyester fibre filling

Using 4.5 mm knitting needles and 2 strands of dark grey DK (8-ply) wool, cast on 46 sts.
Work 3 rows of k1, p1 rib.
Working in loop stitch, and continuing with double strands, follow stripe pattern at the same time.

Loop Stitch

Row 1: Using dark grey, *K1 tbl, p1 tbl, rep from * to last st, p1 tbl.
Row 2: K1, p1, *k1 tbl but do not slip stitch off the left-hand needle. Insert the tip of the right-hand needle into the front of the same stitch and knit the stitch by passing the yarn anti-clockwise around the index finger of the left hand and then around the needle. Slip the stitch off the left-hand needle. Insert the tip of the left-hand needle through the front of the two stitches just worked and knit them together. Pull the loop gently to tighten the knot. Purl next st, rep from * to last 2 sts, k1 tbl, p1.
These 2 rows form the pattern.

Work the **Stripe Pattern** below once:
2 rows dark grey.
2 rows chocolate.
2 rows dark grey.
2 rows rust.
2 rows dark grey.
2 rows beige.
2 rows dark grey.
2 rows cream.
2 rows dark grey.
2 rows beige.
2 rows dark grey.
2 rows rust.
2 rows dark grey.

Commence Decrease

Row 1: Rib 3, *k2tog, rib 2, rep from * to last 3 sts, rib 3.
Row 2: K1, *k2tog, p1, rep from * to last 2 sts, k2tog.
Row 3: P1, *p2tog, all across.
Break off yarn, thread through rem sts. Pull up tightly and fasten off.
Make 2.

To Make Up The Cosy Sew in all loose ends.
With right sides together, join top and down each side for 4–5 cm and up from bottom edge for 3–4 cm. Turn right side out.

TOP KNOT

Using 3 x 2.75 mm double-pointed knitting needles and 1 strand rust, cast on 15 sts (5, 5, 5).
Work 5 rounds rust.
Work 5 rounds chocolate.
Work 5 rounds beige.
Work 5 rounds cream.
Round 21: K1, sl1, k2tog, psso, on each needle, using cream.
Work 4 rounds cream.
Continue in cream.
Round 26: K1, sl1, k1, psso, on each needle.
Work 4 rounds.
Round 31: K2 tog all round.
Cont as an I-cord for another 10 cm. Fasten off.

Stuff firmly with polyester fibre filling and then centre on the top of the tea cosy. Stitch in place so that it stands firmly upright. Knot the end.

Daffodils and Jonquils

This is a tea cosy for spring days with its cheerful knitted bright yellow and orange daffodils and smaller soft yellow jonquils. The toned colours of the leaves and flowers are complemented by a row of felt balls stitched around the bottom of the cosy. The knitted flowers are straightforward to make.

SIZE
To fit a 6-cup teapot

MATERIALS
4 x 50 g balls cream DK (8-ply) wool
Small amounts of DK (8-ply) wool in orange and yellow
Small amounts of 4-ply in orange, yellow and pale yellow
Green 4-ply cotton
1 pair of 4.5mm knitting needles
1 pair 2.25 mm knitting needles
1 pair 2 mm knitting needles
Wool needle
2 packets of Arbee felt balls (approximately 36)

Using 4.5 mm knitting needles and 2 strands of yarn, cast on 46 sts.

Row 1: K1, p1, *k2, p2, rep from * to last 2 sts, p1, k1.

Row 2:*K2, p2, rep from * to end.

These 2 rows form rib pattern.

Continue in rib pattern until work measures 17 cm from beg.

Shape Top

Row 1: K1, p1, *k2, p2tog, rep from * to last 4 sts, k2, p1, k1.

Row 2: K2, *p2, k1 rep from * to last 4 sts, p2, k2.

Row 3: K1, p1, *k2tog, p1, rep from * to last st, k1.

Row 4: K2, p1, *k1, p1, rep from * to last 2 sts, k2.

Row 5: *Sl1, k1, psso, rep from * to last st, k1.

Row 6: K1, purl to last st, k1.

Row 7: K1, k2tog to last st, k1 (7 sts).

Row 8: As row 6.

Row 9: K1, k2tog 3 times.

Break off yarn, thread through rem sts, pull up tightly and fasten off.

Make 2.

To Make Up Body Cosy With right sides together, stitch the top closed for 5 cm down each side. Stitch up from the lower edge for 4 cm, leaving openings for the handle and the spout. Turn right side out.

DAFFODILS AND JONQUILS

Daffodils are knitted in DK (8-ply) on 2.25 mm knitting needles and jonquils are knitted in 4-ply yarn on 2 mm knitting needles.

Cast on 10 sts for the first petal.

Row 1: Sl1, k9.

Row 2: P7.

Row 3: K5.

Row 4: P4.

Row 5: K6.

Row 6: P8, P2tog.

Row 7: Cast off 7 sts, turn, cast on 8 sts (10 sts).

Repeat last 7 rows another 4 times, Cast off.

Trumpet

Using 2.25 mm knitting needles and contrasting orange or yellow colour, cast on 12 sts.

Commencing with a knit row, work 6 rows st st.

Row 7: K1, inc in next st, k3, inc in next st, k3, inc in next st, k2.

Row 8: Purl.

Cast off in k1, p1 rib.

To Make Up Flowers For petals, join centre of cast-on and cast-off points together and gather the centre.

To make the trumpet, with right sides together join row ends. Turn right side out. Gather cast-on end. Centre on petal and stitch firmly in position. Make 4 jonquils and 4 daffodils.

LEAVES

Using 2.25 mm knitting needles and green 4-ply cotton, cast on 3 sts.

Row 1: Knit.

Row 2: Inc in first and last sts (5 sts).

Work in garter st (knit every row) until work measures 10 cm.

Next row: K2tog, knit to end.

Rep this row until 3 sts rem.

Next row: Sl2, k1, psso. Fasten off.

TWISTED CORDS

Using 2.25 mm knitting needles and green 4-ply cotton, cast on 25 sts.

Row 1: Inc in every st.

Row 2: Knit.

Cast off purlwise.

Make 2.

Decorating The Cosy Stitch one daffodil securely to the top of the tea cosy. Position the leaves and the twisted cords around this and stitch in place. On each side of the tea cosy pin, then stitch the remaining daffodils and jonquils. (It is much easier to do this with the cosy sitting on the teapot.) Sew one felt ball to each stocking stitch ridge along the bottom of the tea cosy.

Elsie at the Beach

For a summertime celebration, a fun way to immortalise a favourite child and remember a day out, why not make this hilarious beach scene? A small child, wearing bathing suit and beach ring sits atop a beach towel while enjoying an ice cream. A palm tree and several starfish complete the scene.

SIZE
To fit a 6-cup teapot

MATERIALS
2 x 50 g balls bright blue DK (8-ply) wool
2 x 50 g balls variegated blue DK (8-ply) wool
Small amounts of 4-ply in flesh, green, pink, blue, yellow, orange, brown, oatmeal, beige and white
1 pair 4 mm knitting needles
1 pair 2 mm knitting needles
1 pair 3 mm knitting needles
3.5mm crochet hook
Wool needle
Polyester fibre filling

Using 4 mm knitting needles and bright blue DK (8-ply) yarn, cast on 98 sts.
Work 8 rows garter st (every row knit). Join in variegated blue.

Begin Pattern

Note The pleated fabric is created by pulling up the yarn not in use tightly across the wrong side on each row. Carry the yarn right across to the ends of the work. It may seem slow to begin with but you will develop a rhythm.

Row 1: K1 bright blue (A), k6 variegated blue (B) *k7A, k7B, rep from * to last 7 sts, k6A, k1B. As you knit, pull the yarn not in use very firmly behind, to draw up the pleats.

Row 2: K1B, k6A, *k7B, k6A, rep from * to last 7 sts, k6B, k1A. Keep yarn to the front in this row and continue to pull the yarn not in use tightly so that the pleats remain firm.

These 2 rows form patt. Continue in patt until 48 rows have been worked.

Commence Decrease with right side facing:

Row 1: K2togA, k3B, k2togA, *k2togA, k3A, k2togB, k3A, k2togB, rep from * to last 7 sts, k2togA, k3B, k2togB.

Row 2: K1B, k4A, *k5B, k5A, rep from * to last 5 sts, k4B, k1A.

Row 3: K2togA, k1B, k2togB, *k2togA, k1A, k2togA, k2togB, k1B, k2togB rep from * to last 5 sts, k2togA, k1A, k2togB.

Row 4: K1B, k2A, *k3B, k3A, rep from * to last 3 sts, k2B, k1A.

Row 5: K2togA, k1B, *k2togA, k1A, k2tog B, k1B, rep from * to last 3 sts, k2tog A, k1B.

Row 6: K1B, k1A, *k2B, k2A, rep from *to last

2 sts, k1B, k1M.

Row 7: K2togA twice, *k2togB, k2togA, rep from * to last 4 sts, (k2togB) twice.

Break off yarn, thread through rem sts, pull up tightly and fasten off.
Make another piece to match.

To Make Up The Cosy Darn in any loose ends. With right sides together, stitch from the centre top down each side for 5 cm. Reinforce the stitching at the top of the spout and handles. Stitch each side together at the bottom edge for 3–4 cm. Turn right side out.

GIRL

Using 2 mm knitting needles and flesh 4-ply, cast on 10 sts for the first leg.

Row 1: Inc into every st (20 sts).
Beginning with a purl row, work 12 rows st st. Leave these sts on a spare needle and make another leg to match.
With right side facing, knit across the 20 sts and then the 20 st on the spare needle (40 sts).
Beginning with a purl row, work 17 rows st st.

Next row: K3, k2tog (3 times), k10, k2tog (3 times), k9.

Next row: Purl.
Work 2 rows st st.

Next row: K9, inc in each of next 3 sts, k10, inc in each of next 3 sts, k9.
Work another 19 rows st st.

Next row: *K2, k2tog, rep from * to end.

Next and alt rows: Purl.

Next row: *K1, k2tog, rep from * to end.

Next row: P2tog all across.
Break off yarn, thread through rem sts, pull up

tightly and fasten off.

FLIPPERS

Using 2 mm knitting needles and yellow 4-ply, cast on 20 sts.

Row 1: Purl.
Row 2: *K1, inc in next st, rep from * to end.
Work 3 rows st st.
Row 6: K13, inc in next 2 sts, k13, inc in last 2 sts.
Row 7: Purl.
Row 8: Increasing in first st, k15, inc in next 2 sts, k15, inc in last st.
Row 9: Knit
Cast off.
Make 2.

To Make Up The Flippers Fold in half. Stitch bottom of flipper closed and fit on to bottom of Elsie's leg. Stitch into place with small stitches.

BATHING COSTUME

Using 2 mm knitting needles and bright pink 4-ply, cast on 10 sts for top bathers.
Knit 2 rows.
Work 2 rows st st, commencing with a knit row.
Row 5: Sl1, k1, psso, knit to last 2 sts, k2tog.
Row 6: Purl.
Cast off.

Bather Bottoms

Using 2 mm knitting needles and bright pink 4-ply, cast on 20 sts.
Knit 2 rows.
Work 4 rows st st, commencing with a knit row.
Cast off 2 sts at beg of next 2 rows.
Cast off 3 sts at beg of next 2 rows.
Cast off 2 sts at beg of next 2 rows.

Dec 1 st at each end of next row.
Next row: Purl.
Cast on 2 sts at beg of next 2 rows.
Cast on 3 sts at beg of next 2 rows.
Cast on 2 sts at beg of next 2 rows.
Work 4 rows st st, commencing with a knit row.
Next row: Purl.
Next row: Knit.
Cast off.

To Make Up The Bathing Costume Attach the bathing costume on to the girl and then stitch up the sides of the bather bottoms. Stitch the top bathers to the front of the bather bottoms and then take a small length of bright pink yarn and attach it around the top of the bather top and around Elsie's neck.

BATHING CAP

Using 2 mm knitting needles and green 4-ply, cast on 14 sts.
Row 1: Knit.
Row 2: Knit.
Row 3: K11, turn.
Row 4: Knit.
Row 5: K9, turn.
Row 6: Knit to end.
Repeat these rows another 10 times.
Knit 1 row. Cast off.

To Make Up The Bathing Cap Sew the cast-off and on-edges together to form a little cap and pop it on the head.

FLOWERS

Using 2 mm knitting needles, cast on 16 sts.
Knit 1 row.
P2 tog all across.
Break off yarn. Thread through rems sts, pull up tightly and fasten off.
Make 8 in total in orange, pink and navy.

To Make Up The Flowers Join row ends together and form into a neat circle. Sew on to the top of the bathing cap.

SWIMMING RING

Using 2 mm knitting needles and orange 4-ply, cast on 14 sts.
Rows 1 and 2: Knit.
Row 3: K10, turn.
Rows 4 and 5: Knit.
Repeat the last five rows another 20 times.
Knit 1 more row. Cast off.
Sew row ends together. Stuff firmly to make a circular shape. Fit onto middle of body.

ICE CREAM CONE

Using 2 mm knitting needles and beige 4-ply, cast on 13 sts.
Working in garter st, knit 2 rows. Dec 1 st at each end of alt rows until 3 sts rem. Cast off.

Ice Cream

Using 2 mm knitting needles and pink 4-ply, cast on 16 sts.
Work 2 rows st st.
Row 3: K2tog all across.
Break off yarn. Thread through rem sts, pull up tightly and fasten off. Join row ends together.

Darn in ends and form in to a rounded shape. Attach to cone.

To Make Up Ice Cream and Cone Sew row ends together to form into a cone. Push a tiny amount of fibre filling inside to hold its shape. Place ice cream piece on top and add a little more filling to make a rounded ice cream. Stitch closed. Place in girl's hand and stitch into position.

BATHING TOWEL

Using 3 mm knitting needles and blue 4-ply, cast on 18 sts.
Work 2 rows k1, p1 rib.
Join in white 4-ply and work in rows of 2 rows white and 2 rows blue in st st. Work a total of 14 stripes.
Work another 2 rows k1, p1 rib in blue. Cast off in rib.

To Make Up Bathing Towel Darn in ends.
Centre towel on the top of the tea cosy.
Centre girl on the top of the towel. Stitch into her chubby legs to secure her so that she remains seated.

PALM TREE

Using 4 mm knitting needles and 1 strand of oatmeal and 1 strand of brown together, cast on 16 sts.
Row 1: Knit.
Row 2: K2, k2tog to end.
Knit another 20 rows garter st. Cast off.

To Make Up Palm Tree Roll up tightly and stitch

seam closed. The bottom edge will be slightly wider than the top.

LEAVES

Using 3.5 mm crochet hook and 1 strand of light green and 1 strand of bright green together, make 14 ch, miss 1ch, 1dbl, 10tr, 1dbl, sl st into last ch. Finish off. Make 6.

To Make Up Leaves Attach the points of the 6 leaves to the top of the trunk.
Securely sew the palm tree to the top of the tea cosy using small stitches.

STARFISH

Using 2.25 mm knitting needles and pale blue, cast on 4 sts.
Row 1: (right side) Inc in each st (8 sts).
Row 2: Knit.
Row 3: K1, (m1, k1) 7 times (15 sts).
Row 4: Knit.
Row 5: K1, m1 (k3, m1) 4 times, K2 (20 sts).
Row 6: Knit.
Row 7: K1, m1, (k2, m1) 9 times, k1 (30 sts).
Row 8: Knit.
**Row 9: K3, m1, k3, turn, continue on these 7 sts.
Rows 10, 11 and 12: Knit.
Row 13: K2, sl2, k1, psso, k2 (5 sts).
Rows 14, 15 and 16: Knit.
Row 17: K1, sl2, k1, psso, k1 (3 sts).
Rows 18, 19 and 20: Knit.
Row 21: Sl2, k1, psso (1 st).
Fasten off.
Rejoining yarn each time, repeat from ** 4 times more. Make 5.

To Make Up Starfish Gather cast-on edge and then join the first 8 rows. Attach the starfish evenly around the tea cosy.

Feathered Finery

This is a striking tea cosy and will look stunning with a black and red tea set. The fancy yarn around the base imitates the fine and frivolous decorative detail of an evening gown and the fabulous fancy feathers provide an unusual crowning glory.

SIZE
To fit a 6-cup teapot

MATERIALS
1 x 50 g ball fancy yarn, red
2 x 50 g balls red DK (8-ply) wool
2 x 50 g balls black DK (8-ply) wool
2 packets of red feathers (www.sullivans.net)
1 pair 4 mm knitting needles
2 x 2.75 mm double-pointed knitting needles
Wool needle
Polyester sewing thread
Sewing needle

Using 4 mm knitting keedles and red fancy yarn, cast on 50 sts.

Work 8 rows garter st (every row knit). Break off fancy yarn and join in red DK (8-ply) (Colour A).

Inc row: K1, *inc in each st, rep from * to last st, k1 (98 sts). Join in black DK (8-ply) (Colour B).

Begin Pattern

Note The pleated fabric is created by pulling the yarn not in use tightly across the wrong side on each row. Carry the yarn right across to the ends of the work. It may seem a little slow to begin with but you will develop a rhythm.

Row 1: K1A, k6B, *k7A, k7B, rep from * to last 7 sts, k6A, k1B. As you knit, pull the yarn not in use very firmly behind to draw up the pleats.

Row 2: K1B, k6A, *k7B, k6A, rep from * to last 7 sts, k6B, k1A. Keep yarn to the front in this row and continue to pull the yarn not in use tightly so that the pleats remain firm.

These 2 rows form patt. Continue in patt until 48 rows have been worked.

Commence Decrease with Right Side Facing

Row 1: K2togA, k3B, k2togB, *k2tog A, k3A, k2togB, k3B, k2togB, rep from * to last 7 sts, k2togA, k3A, k2togB.

Row 2: K1B, k4A, *k5B, k5A, rep from * to last 5 sts, k4B, k1A.

Row 3: K2togA, k1B, k2togB, *k2tog A, k1A, k2tog A, k2togB, k1B, k2togB rep from * to last 5 sts, k2togA, k1A, k2togB.

Row 4: K1B, k2A, *k3B, k3A, rep from * to last 3 sts, k2B, k1A.

Row 5: K2togA, k1B, *k2togA, k1A, k2togB, k1B, rep from * to last 3 sts, k2togA, k1B.

Row 6: K1B, k1A, *k2B, k2A, rep from *to last 2 sts, k1B, k1A.

Row 7: K2togA twice, *k2togB, k2togA, rep from * to last 4 sts, (k2togB) twice.

Break off yarn, thread through rem sts, pull up tightly and fasten off.

Make 2.

To Make Up The Cosy Darn in any loose ends. With right sides together, stitch from the centre top down each side for 5 cm. Reinforce the stitching at the end point. Join sides together at the bottom edge, stitching up each side for 3–4 cm. Turn right side out.

I-CORD CENTREPIECE

Using 2.75 mm double-pointed knitting needles and red fancy yarn, cast on 3 sts.

Knit 1 row. Do not turn. *Slide sts to other end of needle and pull yarn firmly behind work. K3, rep from * until cord is 10 cm long.

Sl2, k1, psso. Fasten off.

Form into a ring and place on the top of the tea cosy. Stitch firmly in place. Place the feathers in the centre of the ring. Sew them carefully maintaining an upright position using polyester sewing thread.

Felted Flowers

This tea cosy makes a good project for a less experienced knitter. The cosy is knitted in two pieces using a knit and purl rib and knits up fairly quickly. The decorations are felted flowers, which are widely available in craft stores. The trick is to be lavish in your use of them and don't use just one or two. Have a whole flower garden on your tea cosy. Sew them on invisibly and you will achieve a really professional finish. An over-the-top I-cord daisy adds the perfect finishing touch.

SIZE
To fit a 6-cup teapot

MATERIALS
4 x 50 g balls bright pink DK (8-ply) wool
1 pair 4.5 mm knitting needles
2 x 2.75 mm double-pointed knitting needles
Wool needle
40 felt flowers
Polyester sewing cotton
Sewing needle
1 x 8 mm pink felt ball

Using 4.5 mm knitting needles and 2 strands of bright pink yarn, cast on 46 sts.

Row 1: K1, p1, *k2, p2, rep from * to last 2 sts, p1, k1.

Row 1: *K2, p2, rep from * to end.

These 2 rows form rib pattern.

Continue in rib pattern until work measure 17 cm from beg.

Shape Top

Row 1: K1, p1, *k2, p2tog, rep from * to last 4 sts, k2, p1 k1.

Row 2: K2, *p2, k1 rep from * to last 4 sts, p2, k2.

Row 3: K1, p1, *k2tog, p1, rep from * to last st, k1.

Row 4: K2 ,p1, *k1, p1, rep from * to last 2 sts, k2.

Row 5: *Sl1, k1, psso, rep from * to last st, k1.

Row 6: K1, purl to last st, k1.

Row 7: K1, k2tog to last st, k1 (7 sts).

Row 8: As row 6.

Row 9: K1, k2tog 3 times.

Break off yarn, thread through rem sts, pull up tightly and fasten off.

Make 2.

To Make Up The Cosy With right sides of cosy together, stitch the top closed for approximately 5 cm down each side. Stitch up from the lower edge for 4 cm, leaving an opening for the handle and the spout. Turn right side out.

Put the cosy on the teapot so that it is slightly stretched. This gives a better surface to work on. Pin the felt flowers on in a random manner, checking the colours as you go. Once you are happy with the look, sew in place using polyester thread. Take a few stitches to secure the thread to the underside of the cosy, then bring the needle out through the flower. Make a few holding stitches in the same place.

I-CORD DAISY

Using 2.75 mm double-pointed knitting needles and pink DK (8-ply), make an I cord 50 cm long. Fasten off. Fold into five even petals, leaving a short length of stem. Secure to the top centre of the flower using small stitches. Place the felt ball on top. Sew in place.

Giant Cables

Practise your cable stitch on this small-scale, neatly fitting tea cosy. The pattern looks complicated but is surprisingly easy to achieve; the trick is to keep checking that the cables are following the correct direction. A contrast blanket stitch decoration around spout and handle openings and a loopy I-cord decoration on the body of the cosy complete the embellishments.

SIZE
To fit a 6-cup teapot

MATERIALS
3 x 50 g balls of bright blue Twilleys Freedom Wool
1 x 50 g ball purple DK (8-ply) wool
Small amount of cream DK (8-ply) wool
1 x 8 mm purple felt ball
1 pair 4.5 mm knitting needles
2 x 2.25 mm double-pointed knitting needles
2 x 2.75 mm double-pointed knitting needles
Wool needle

CABLE ABBREVIATIONS

Cr3L: Sl2 sts on to cable needle and hold at front of work, p1, then k2 from cable needle.

Cr3R: Sl1 st on to cable needle and hold at back of work, k2, then p1 from cable needle.

C4F: Sl2 sts on to cable needle and hold at front of work, k2, then k2 from cable needle.

C4B: Sl2 sts on to cable needle and hold at back of work, k2 and then k2 from cable needle.

Using 4.5 mm knitting needles and bright blue wool, cast on 46 sts.
Work 4 rows garter st (every row knit).

Commence Cable Pattern

Worked over 8 rows

Row 1: P9, Cr3L, Cr3R, Cr3L, p4, k3, p4, Cr3L, Cr3R, Cr3L, p8.

Rows 2, 4 and 6: Knit all knit sts and purl all purl sts as they appear.

Row 3: P10, C4B, p2, k2, p4, k3, p5, C4B, p2, k2, p8.

Row 5: P9, Cr3R, Cr3L, Cr3R, p4, k3, p4, Cr3R, Cr3L, Cr3R, p8.

Row 7: P9, k2, p3, C4F, p1, p4, k3, p4, k2, p3, C4F, p9.

Row 8: K9, p4, k2, p2, k4, p3, k5, p4, k2, p2, k9.
These 8 rows for pattern. Repeat pattern another three times.

Shape Top

Next row: P2. p2tog, p2, p2tog, p1, k2tog, p2tog, k2tog, k2tog, p2tog, p2, p2tog, p2, sl1, k2tog, psso, p4, k2tog, p2tog, k2tog, k2tog, p2tog, p2, p2tog, p2.

Next row: Knit all knit sts and purl all purl sts as they appear.

Next row: P1, p2tog (3 times), k2tog (twice), p2tog (twice), k1, p2tog (twice), k2tog (2 times), p2tog (3 times), p1.

Next row: Knit all knit sts and purl all purl sts as they appear.

Next row: Knit all knit sts and purl all purl sts as they appear.

Next row: P2tog (twice), k2tog, p2tog, k1, p2tog, k2tog, p2tog (2 times).

Next row: Purl.

Break off yarn, thread through rem sts, pull up tightly and fasten off.
Make 2.

To Make Up The Cosy With right sides together join pieces at centre top and for 4–5 cm down each side. Stitch from the bottom edge up for 3–4 cm. Darn in all ends.
Using purple, work a row of blanket stitch around the spout and handle openings.

I-CORD SWIRLS

For loopy swirls, make 2 I-cords, each 40 cm long, using 2.25 mm knitting needles. Make 1 in purple and 1 in cream.
Pin one end of the cord to the bottom of the stocking stitch panel in the centre of the tea cosy and form a small loop. Pin three more loops evenly all the way up the panel. Stitch in place. Repeat for the other side.

I-CORD FLOWERS

For the centre top flowers make 1 purple
I-cord, 50 cm long, using 2.75 mm double-
pointed knitting needles. Fasten off. Fold into
5 even petals, leaving a short length of stem.
Secure firmly using small stitches at the centre
of the flower to keep the shape. Make a second
I-cord 40 cm long using cream and fold into a
similar flower, but with slightly smaller petals.
Place the cream flower on top of the purple
flower and stitch in place.
Sew the felt ball in the middle. Sew the flower
securely to the top of the tea cosy.

Hop, Hop, One Happy Frog

No collection of tea cosies would be complete without one decorated with a frog. This one is sitting on top of a leaf surrounded by daisies and water. Take your time making the frog as the parts are small, but your patience will pay off because he is as cute as pie, and undoubtedly a great asset to any tea party.

SIZE
To fit a 6-cup teapot

MATERIALS
2 x 50 g balls of blue DK (8-ply) wool
2 x 50 g balls of mid-green DK (8-ply) wool
Small amount of DK (8-ply) in cream, yellow, sage green and bright green
Small amount of green Dolce Amore 4-ply cotton
Black embroidery thread
Polyester fibre filling
Wool needle
Embroidery needle
1 pair 4.5 mm knitting needles
2 x 2.75 mm double-pointed knitting needles
4 x 2.25 mm double-pointed knitting needles
3 mm crochet hook

Using 4.5 mm knitting needles and 2 strands of mid-green DK (8-ply) wool, cast on 46 sts.

Row 1: K1, p1, *k2, p2, rep from * to last 2 sts, p1, k1.

Row 2: *K2, p2, rep from * to end.

These 2 rows form rib pattern.

Work 10 rows mid-green.

Work 10 rows blue.

Work 11 rows mid green.

Work 5 rows blue.

Shape Top

Row 1: Continuing in blue, k1, p1, *k2, p2tog, rep from * to last 4 sts, k2, p1, k1.

Row 2: K2, *p2, k1 rep from * to last 4 sts, p2, k2.

Row 3: K1, p1, *k2tog, p1, rep from * to last st, k1.

Row 4: K2, p1, *k1, p1, rep from * to last 2 sts, k2.

Row 5: *Sl1, k1, psso, rep from * to last st, k1.

Row 6: K1, purl to last st, k1.

Row 7: K1, k2tog to last st, k1 (7 sts).

Row 8: As row 6.

Row 9: K1, k2tog 3 times.

Break off yarn, thread through rem sts, pull up tightly and fasten off. Make 2.

To Make Up The Cosy With right sides of cosy together, stitch the top closed for 5 cm down each side. Stitch up from the lower edge for 4 cm leaving an opening for the handle and the spout. Turn right side out.

FROG

Using 2.25 mm double-pointed knitting needles and Dolce Amore, cast on 9 sts (3, 3, 3). Form into a circle, being careful not to twist the ring.

Round 1: Knit.

Round 2: *K1, m1, rep from * to end of round (15 sts).

Work 4 rounds st st without shaping.

Round 7: *Sl1, k1, psso, k1, k2tog, rep from * to end (9 sts).

Round 8: Knit.

Leave sts on needle. Stuff head firmly to make a round shape, then thread yarn through rem sts, pull up tightly and fasten off.

BODY

Using 2.25 mm double-pointed knitting needles and Dolce Amore, cast on 9 sts (3, 3, 3). Form into a circle, being careful not to twist the ring.

Round 1: Knit.

Round 2: *K1, m1, rep from * to end of round (15 sts).

Work 4 rounds st st without shaping.

Round 7: Knit.

Round 8: *K1, m1, k3, m1, k1, rep from * to end (21 sts).

Work 4 rounds st st without shaping.

Round 9: *Sl1, k1, psso, k3, k2tog, rep from * to end (15 sts).

Round 10: Knit.

Round 11: *Sl1, k1, psso, k1, k2tog, rep from * to end (9 sts).

Round 12: Knit.

Leaving sts on needle, stuff body firmly to make a round shape. Thread yarn through rem sts, pull up tightly and fasten off.

Legs and Arms

Using 2 x 2.25 mm double-pointed knitting

needles and Dolce Amore, cast on 2 sts. Make an I-cord for 3 cm. Sl2, k1, psso. Fasten off. Make 4.

Eyes, Feet and Hands

These are made as bobbles and then sewn on to the head or ends of arms or legs.

Using 2.25 mm double-pointed knitting needles and Dolce Amore, cast on 1 st.

Row 1: Knit into the front, back and front of the stitch (3 sts).

Row 2: Knit.

Row 3: Purl.

Row 4: Knit – don't turn work, pass second, third and fourth sts one at a time over the first st. Fasten off. Run a gathering thread around the outside and pull up to from a bobble. Make 6.

To Make Up The Frog Sew head firmly to body. Position arms at shoulders and stitch in place. Position legs on each side of the body and stitch in place. Sew a hand or a foot bobble onto the end of each arm and leg. Stitch the eyes carefully to the top of the head. Work a French knot in black embroidery thread in the centre of each eye. Give your frog a lovely big smile by taking a wide stitch across the centre of his face and anchoring with a tiny stitch in the centre. Fasten off under the body.

FLOWERS

Using 3 mm crochet hook and yellow DK (8-ply) make 6ch, form into a loop with a sl st. Work 1ch, then 7dc into the loop. Sl st into first dc.

Break off yellow and join in cream DK (8-ply). Make *7ch, sl st into next dc, rep from * until 12 petals have been completed. Fasten off. Make 8 daisies.

Note It is easier to attach the daises if you pop your cosy on to the teapot first.

LEAVES

Using 2.75 mm double-pointed knitting needles and dk (8 ply), cast on 3 sts. Work an 'I' Cord for 1.5 cm for leaf stem. Continuing on, k1 row.

Row 2: Knit.

Row 3: K1, m1, k1, m1, k1.

Row 4 and all even rows: Knit.

Row 5: K2, m1, k1, m1, k2.

Row 7: K3, m1, k1, m1, k3.

Row 9: K4, m1, k1, m1, k4.

Row 11: K5, m1, k1, m1, k5.

Rows 13 and 15: Knit.

Row 17: K5, sl2, k1, psso, k5.

Row 19: K4, sl2, k1, psso, k4.

Row 21: K3, sl2, k1, psso, k3.

Row 23: K2, sl2, k1, psso, k2.

Rows 24 and 26: Purl.

Row 25: K1, sl2, k1, psso, k1 (3 sts).

Row 25: K1, sl 2, psso, fasten off.

Make 5: 2 in bright green and 3 in sage green.

To Decorate The Cosy Sew the frog firmly to a sage green leaf. Attach the frog and leaf to the centre top of the cosy. Sew 1 sage green and 1 bright green leaf to each side of the cosy so that the stems protrude. Sew the daisies at random around the cosy.

Liquorice Allsorts

With their simple shapes and multi-colours, knitted-wool liquorice allsorts knitted make a cheerful and zany addition to an all-black tea cosy. Limit the colours for maximum visual zing in this homage to these classic sweet-shop favourites.

SIZE

To fit a 6-cup teapot

MATERIALS

4 x 50 g balls black DK (8 ply) pure wool
Small amount of bright green dk (8 ply)
2 x 2.75 mm double-pointed knitting needles
1 pair of 4.5 mm knitting needles
Wool needle
1 pair 2 mm knitting needles
Small amounts of 4 ply in: black, pink, orange and yellow

Using 4.5 mm knitting needles and black DK (8 ply), cast on 46 sts.

Rib Pattern
Row 1: K1, p1, *k2, p2, rep from * to last 2 sts, p1, k1.
Row 2: *K2, p2, rep from * to end.
These 2 rows form rib pattern.
Continue in rib until work measure 17 cm from beg.

Shape Top
Row 1: K1, p1, *k2, p2tog, rep from * to last 4 sts, k2, p1, k1.
Row 2: K2, *p2, k1, rep from * to last 4 sts, p2, k2.
Row 3: K1, p1, *k2tog, p1, rep from * to last st, k1.
Row 4: K2, p1, *k1, p1, rep from * to last 2 sts, k2.
Row 5: *Sl1, k1, psso, rep from * to last st, k1.
Row 6: K1, purl to last st, k1.
Row 7: K1, k2tog to last st, k1 (7 sts).
Row 8: As row 6.
Row 9: K1, k2tog 3 times.
Break off yarn, thread through rem sts, pull up tightly and fasten off.
Make 2.

To Make Up The Cosy With right sides of cosy together, and working from centre top out, stitch down each side for 5 cm. Stitch up from the lower edge for 4 cm leaving an opening for the handle and the spout. Turn right side out.

LARGE LIQUORICE ALLSORTS
These are made up of four layers of colour; 2 black, 1 orange and 1 pink.

Using 2 mm knitting needles and black 4-ply, cast on 20 sts. Work 40 rows garter st. Cast off. Make 2. Press.

Coloured Slices
Using 2 mm knitting needles and pink 4-ply, cast on 15 sts. Work 30 rows garter st. Cast off. Make one more with orange 4-ply.

To Make Up The Large Allsorts Fold each corner of each black square into the centre to make a smaller square as if you were creating an envelope. Stitch each diagonal seam. Place a coloured square on top, then a folded black square. Place the last coloured slice on top. Carefully stitch through the layers to hold them together.
Centre the shape on top of the tea cosy. Stitch in place.

SMALL LIQUORICE ALLSORTS
Using 2 mm knitting needles and black 4-ply, cast on 15 sts. Work 30 rows garter st. Cast off. Make 2.

Coloured Slices
Using 2 mm knitting needles and pink 4-ply, cast on 10 sts. Work 20 rows garter stitch. Cast off. Make one more with orange 4-ply.

To Make Up Small Liquorice Allsorts Make up as for large liquorice allsorts.

LIQUORICE ROLLS

Using 2 mm knitting needles and black 4-ply, cast on 6 sts. Work 40 rows. Cast off. Make 2.

Coloured Slices

Using 2 mm knitting needles and pink 4-ply, cast on 6 sts. Work 22 rows grter stitch. Cast off. Make one more with orange 4-ply.

To Make Up Liquorice Rolls Centre one coloured slice on top of a black square and roll up firmly. Stitch closed. Stitch onto the side of the tea cosy. Repeat with the other liquorice roll.

I-CORD KNOTS

Using 2.75 mm knitting needles and bright green 8-ply, cast on 3 sts. Knit 1 row. Do not turn. *Slide sts to other end of needle and pull yarn firmly behind work. Knit 3 sts, rep from * until cord is 10 cm long.

Next row: Sl2, k1, psso. Fasten off. Make 5.

To Decorate The Cosy Stitch the 5 I-cords evenly around the central large allsort. Knot each I-cord.

Mad Hatter

This colourful confection, with its bright pink and orange skirt and delightfully contrasting black and white decorations, inspired, of course, by the Hatter in *Alice In Wonderland,* for whom life is a constant tea party. What better philosophy indeed? Now one white rabbit and one hat for that matter, is never enough, neither one hat, so make as many as you think will fit, or you have patience to create. Take your time with the embellishments to make them all match.

SIZE
To fit a 6-cup teapot

MATERIALS
2 x 50 g balls bright pink DK (8 ply)
2 x 50 g balls orange DK (8 ply)
1 pair 4 mm knitting needles
25 g white 4-ply cotton
25 g black 4-ply wool
15 g orange 4-ply or fancy yarn for rabbits' scarves
Stranded embroidery thread in pink and black
2 x 2.25 mm double-pointed knitting needles
1 pair 2 mm knitting needles
Wool needle
Sewing needle
Polyester fibre filling

Using 4 mm knitting needles and orange DK A (8-ply), cast on 98 sts. Work 8 rows garter st. (every row knit). Join in pink (B)

Row 1: K1A, k6B, *k7A, k7B, rep from * to last 7 sts, k6A, k1B. As you knit pull the yarn not in use very firmly behind, to draw up the pleats.

Row 2: K1B, k6A, *k7B, k6A, rep from * to last 7 sts, k6B, k1A. Keep yarn to the front in this row and continue to pull the yarn not in use tightly so that pleats remain firm.

These 2 rows form pattern. Continue in pattern until 48 rows have been worked.

With rs facing Commence Decreases

Row 1: K2togA, k3B, k2togB, *k2togA, k3A, k2togB, k3B, k2togB, rep from * to last 7 sts, k2togA, k3A, k2togB.

Row 2: K1B, k4A, *k5B, k5A, rep from * to last 5 sts, k4B, k1A.

Row 3: K2togA, k1B, k2togB, *k2togA, k1A, k2togA, k2togB, k1B, k2togB rep from * to last 5 sts, k2togA, k1A, k2togB.

Row 4: K1B, k2A, *k3B, k3A, rep from * to last 3 sts, k2B, k1A.

Row 5: K2togA, k1B, *k2togA, k1MB, k2togB, k1B, rep from * to last 3 sts, k2togA, k1B.

Row 6: K1B, k1A, *k2B, k2A, rep from *to last 2 sts, k1B, k1A.

Row 7: (K2togA) twice, *k2togB, k2togA, rep from * to last 4 sts, (k2togB) twice.

Break off yarn, thread through rem sts, pull up tightly and fasten off.

Make 2.

To Make Up The Cosy Darn in any loose ends.

With right sides together, stitch from the centre top down each side for 5 cm. Tie off very firmly. Stitch

3–4 cm together at the bottom edge. Turn right side out.

RABBIT

Use 4-ply white cotton and 2.25 mm double-pointed knitting needles.

Head

Cast on 9 sts, (3, 3, 3) and join into a ring.

Round 1: Knit.

Round 2: K1, m1, k1, on each needle (15 sts).

Round 3: Knit.

Round 4: K1, m1, k3, m1, k1 (21 sts).

Rounds 5–8: Knit.

Round 9: K1, k2tog, k1, k2tog, k1 (15 sts).

Rounds 10 and 11: Knit.

Round 12: Sl1, k1, psso, k1, k2tog (9 sts).

Round 13: Knit.

Leaving sts on needle, stuff head firmly. Run thread through rem sts, pull up tightly and fasten off. Set aside.

Body

Cast on 9 sts (3, 3, 3). Join into a ring.

Round 1: Knit.

Round 2: K1, m1, k1, on each needle (15 sts).

Round 3: Knit.

Round 4: K1, m1, k3, m1, k1 (21 sts).

Round 5: Knit.

Round 6: K1, m1, k5, m1, k1 (27 sts).

Rounds 7–15: Knit.

Round 16: Sl1, k1, psso, k5, k2tog on each needle (21 sts).

Round 17: Knit.
Round 18: Sl1, k1, psso, k3, k2tog, on each needle (15 sts).
Round 19: Knit.
Round 20: Sl1, k1, psso, k1, k2tog, on each needle (9 sts).
Round 21: Knit.
Leaving sts on needle, stuff body firmly. Run thread through rem sts, pull up tightly and fasten off. Set aside.

Ears

Using 2.25 mm double-pointed knitting needles and working backwards and forwards in rows, cast on 2 sts.
Row 1 and all odd rows: Purl.
Row 2: K1, m1, k1.
Row 4: K1, m1, k1, m1, k1.
Work 15 rows st st ending with a purl row.
Next row: K2tog, k1, k2tog.
Next row: Purl.
Cast off. Make 2.

I-Cord Legs and Arms

Make 2 arms, each 3 cm long, and 2 legs, each 4 cm long.
Using 2.25 mm double-pointed knitting needles and white 4-ply cotton, cast on 3 sts.
Knit 1 row. Do not turn, slide sts to the other end of the needle, pull yarn firmly behind the work and repeat the first row. Continue in this manner until your I-cord is the desired length.
To finish, sl1, k2tog, psso, fasten off.

Feet, Paws and Tail

Cast on 1 st.
Knit, purl, knit, purl, knit, into this stitch (5 sts).

Turn. Purl. Turn. Knit. Turn. Purl. Turn. Knit. Do not turn, Slip the second stitch over the first stitch on the right-hand needle. Continue in this manner until 1 st remains. Break off yarn. Thread through st. Pull up tightly and fasten off. To form into a bobble, run a gathering stitch around the outside, draw up and fasten off, forming into a good circular shape. Attach one to each arm and leg and keep one for the tail.

To Make Up The Rabbits Sew head to body with pointy nose facing forwards. Pin ears to each side of head and sew in place.
Using 3 strands of pink embroidery cotton work a few short stitches across and one or two down for the nose.
To embroider the eyes, use 3 strands of black stranded cotton and work a couple of short stitches or make a French knot. Tie off where the body attaches to the head so the knot will be hidden.
Firmly stitch a leg to each side of lower body and one arm to each side of upper body.

Scarf

Using 2.25 mm double-pointed knitting needles and working backwards and forwards in rows, cast on 3 sts in orange 4-ply.
Work in k1, p1 rib for 11 cm. Cast off.
Darn in ends.

HAT

Use 2 mm knitting needles and black 4-ply.
Make 8 hats.
Hat Brim

Cast on 51 sts for the brim.
Row 1: Purl.
Row 2: *K2, inc in next st, rep from * to end
(68 sts).
Beg with a purl row, work 4 rows st st.
Row 7: Purl.
Beg with a purl row, work 6 rows st st.
Row 14: *P2, p2tog, rep from * to end.
Row 15: Knit.
Cast off.

Crown

Cast on 45 sts.
Work 8 rows st st.
Row 9: Purl.
Work another 14 rows st st beg with a purl row.

Shape Hat Top

Row 1: *K3, k2tog, rep from * to end.
Row 2 and all even rows: Purl.
Row 3: *K2, k2tog, rep from * to end.
Row 5: *K1, k2tog, rep from * to end.
Row 7: K2tog all across.
Break off yarn, thread through rem sts, pull up
tightly and fasten off.

To Make Up The Hat Shape With right sides
together, join the row ends of the brim.
Folded the crown lining to the inside.
Place the brim over the crown and stitch to the
lower edge of the crown.

Hat Band

Using 2.25 mm double-pointed knitting needles
and orange 4-ply, cast on 3 sts. Work an I-cord,
long enough to fit around the base of the hat.
Fasten off.

Stitch in place.
Make 8.

To Make Up The Hat Fill each hat firmly with
polyester fibre filling. Position on tea cosy and
move about until you are happy. Then stitch in
place around the bottom of the crown so no
filling leaks out.
Arrange the rabbits around the hats and stitch
in place.

Madly Marguerite

The combination of blue, white and yellow used on this attractive tea cosy is comfortable and cheerful at the same time. The basic pattern is knitted in two pieces and knits up quickly in chunky wool. The marguerite daisies are crocheted separately and then applied to the cosy once they are all complete. The more daisies you cover your cosy with, the better it will look.

SIZE
To fit a 6-cup teapot

MATERIALS
2 x 50 g balls of blue chunky
    (12-ply) or DK (8-ply) wool
1 x 50 g ball cream DK
    (8-ply) wool
1 x 50 g ball yellow DK
    (8-ply) wool
1 pair 4 mm knitting needles
3 mm crochet hook
Wool needle

Note 8-ply size is given in brackets

Using 4 mm knitting needles, cast on 46 sts (12-ply) or 54 sts (8-ply)

Beginning with a knit row, work 6 (8) rows st st.

Picot edge row: K1, *yfwd, k2tog, rep from * to last 2 sts, k2.

Beginning with a purl row, work another 7 (9) rows st st.

Row 15: Wth right side facing, fold up hem at picot edge and knit 1 st together with loop from cast-on edge until all sts have been worked.

Commence Pattern

Row 1: Knit.

Row 2 and all even rows: Purl.

Row 3: P1, *k, p, k into same st, p3tog, rep from * to last st, p1.

Row 5: P1, *p3tog, k, p, k into same st, rep from * to last st, p1.

Row 6: Purl.

These 5 rows form pattern.

Continue in patt until work measures 17 cm from picot edge and ending with row 6.

Commence Decrease

Next row: P1, *p1, p3tog, rep from * to end.

Next row: K2tog all across.

Break off yarn thread through rem sts. Pull up tightly and fasten off.

Make 2.

To Make Up The Cosy With right sides together carefully stitch the top seam closed, from the centre point 5–6 cm down each side. Turn right side out.

Handle and Spout Openings

Using 4 mm knitting needles and chunky (12-ply) or DK (8-ply) wool, and with the right side facing, pick up and knit 48 (55) sts along both pieces. Work 12 rows st st. Cast off.

To Make Up The Openings Fold piece to the wrong side and carefully stitch in place. Join the bottom seam for 3–4 cm.

Sew in any loose ends.

MARGUERITE DAISIES

Using 3 mm crochet hook and yellow DK (8-ply), make 6ch. Form into a loop with a sl st.

Work 1ch, then 11dc into the loop formed. Sl st into 1st dc.

Break off yellow and join in cream dk (8 ply).

Make *11 ch, sl st into next dc, rep from * until 12 petals have been completed. Fasten off. Make as many daisies as you need to cover the cosy.

Note It is easier to attach the daises if you pop your cosy on to the teapot first.

Maybe a Ladybird

The bold red and black of this design gives the impression of a ladybird, particularly if you have a very rounded teapot on which to model your tea cosy. The ladybird spots are knitted balls, which are stuffed to a firm shape.

SIZE
To fit a 6-cup teapot

MATERIALS
4 x 50 g balls red DK (8-ply) wool
1 x 50 g ball black DK (8-ply) wool
Small amount black 4-ply wool
1 pair 4.5 mm knitting needles
2 x 2.25 mm double-pointed knitting needles
2 x 3 mm double-pointed knitting needles
Wool needle
Polyester fibre filling

Using 4.5 mm knitting keedles and red, cast on 46 sts.

Row 1: K1, p1, *k2, p2, rep from * to last 2 sts, p1, k1.

Row 2: *K2, p2, rep from * to end.

These 2 rows form rib pattern.

Continue in rib until work measure 17 cm from cast-on edge.

Shape Top

Row 1: K1, p1, *k2, p2tog, rep from * to last 4 sts, k2, p1, k1.

Row 2: K2, *p2, k1 rep from * to last 4 sts, p2, k2.

Row 3: K1, p1, *k2tog, p1, rep from * to last st, k1.

Row 4: K2, p1, *k1, p1, rep from * to last 2 sts, k2.

Row 5: *Sl1, k1, psso, rep from * to last st, k1.

Row 6: K1, purl to last st, k1.

Row 7: K1, k2tog to last st, k1 (7 sts).

Row 8: As row 6.

Row 9: K1, k2tog 3 times.

Break off yarn, thread through rem sts, pull up tightly and fasten off.

Make 2.

To Make Up The Cosy With right sides together, stitch the top closed for 5 cm down each side. Stitch up from the lower edge for 4 cm leaving an opening for the handle and the spout. Turn right side out.

LADYBIRD SPOTS

Using 3 mm knitting needles and black DK (8-ply), cast on 12 sts.

Row 1: Knit.

Row 2: P10, wrap.

Row 3: K8, wrap.

Row 4: P6, wrap.

Row 5: K4, wrap.

Row 6: Purl.

Rep these 6 rows another 4 times. Cast off. With right sides together, sew side seam half way. Turn right side out and stuff firmly. Sew the rest of the seam and then run a gathering thread around the cast-on edge. Pull up firmly and fasten off. Do the same with the other end. Make sure you have sufficient filling and the balls are firm. Make 4.

Make 2 small balls using 2.25mm double-pointed knitting needles and black 4-ply wool following the instructions above.

Pin 2 large and 2 small balls to each side of the cosy. Stitch firmly in position. It is easier to do this with the cosy on the teapot as it provides a firm surface to work on.

Old-fashioned Paintbox

This tea cosy is reminiscent of childhood watercolour paint sets with their rows of different coloured paint tablets. The cosy is made by making mitred squares and knitting them together in rows. A plain stocking stitch lining adds extra thickness and warmth and also creates a very neat finish, hiding all the wool ends. Use as many different colours as you like.

SIZE
To fit a 6-cup teapot

MATERIALS
Small quantities of the
    following colours in DK
    (8-ply) wool: blue, variegated
    orange/pink, purple, jade,
    red, variegated blue/green,
    green, pink, orange, yellow,
    and purple fleck.
2 x 50 g balls of chunky (12-ply)
    navy blue wool
1 pair 4 mm knitting needles
2 x 4 mm double-pointed
    knitting needles
Wool needle

Each side is made of 20 squares. Mix and match your colours for maximum contrast – colour code a little diagram first if it will help.

MITRED SQUARES

Using 4 mm knitting needles and first colour cast on 25 sts.

Row 1: K1tbl, k10, k3tog, k10, slip last st wyif.
Row 2 and all even rows: K1tbl, knit to last st, slip last st wyif.
Row 3: K1tbl, k9, k3tog, k9, slip last st wyif.
Row 5: K1tbl, k8, k3tog, k8, slip last st wyif.
Row 7: K1tbl, k7, k3tog, k7, slip last st wyif.
Row 9: K1tbl, k6, k3tog, k6, slip last st wyif.
Row 11: K1tbl, k5, k3tog, k5, slip last st wyif.
Row 13: K1tbl, k4, k3tog, k4, slip last st wyif.
Row 15: K1tbl, k3, k3tog, k3, slip last st wyif.
Row 17: K1tbl, k2, k3tog, k2, slip last st wyif.
Row 19: K1tbl, k1, k3tog, k1, slip last st wyif.
Row 21: K1tbl, k3tog, slip last st wyif.
Row 23: K3tog. Break off yarn, Thread through rem st and fasten off. Darn in ends.

With second choice of colour, pick up and knit 12 sts along one side from the bottom left corner of the square. Turn and cast on 13 sts (25 sts). Knit the second square as for the first square. Continue in this manner until you have a row of 5 squares in contrasting colours.
For the first square on the second row pick up 12 stitches along the top of the first square. Complete as for the first row. At the end of the second row of 5 squares, sew the rows together. Continue in this manner until you have 4 rows of 5 squares knitted or sewn together.
Darn in all ends.

Make 2.

LINING

Using 4 mm knitting needles and chunky (12-ply) navy blue yarn, cast on 55 sts. Work 4 rows garter st. Continue in st st until piece is the same length as the outer casing. Cast off. Make 2.

To Make Up The Cosy Pin a lining piece to an outer casing with wrong sides together and ensuring that the garter stitch border of the lining is on the lower edge. Stitch in place all round. Repeat for the remaining pieces. With the lining facing out, stitch the two halves together along the top seam and down each side for 1 square. Sew the lower edges for slightly more than half a square. Turn right side out.

I-CORD LOOP

Using a pair of 4 mm double-pointed knitting needles and two strands of chunky (12-ply) navy blue yarn, cast on 3 sts and make an I-cord 20 cm long. Fasten off.

To Decorate The Cosy Fold the loop in half and stitch firmly to the top centre of the tea cosy.

Mystic Meg

Tiny decorative charms are built into this tea cosy, giving a suitable magical, gemstone aura to the Mystic Meg character. Her body is a knitted ball and she has one beaded arm and leg and one I-cord arm and leg. Felted flowers and large beads complete the decoration on this simple ribbed cosy.

MATERIALS

1 pair 4.5 mm knitting needles

4 x 50 g balls of purple DK (8-ply) wool

2 x 2.75 mm double-pointed knitting needles

Small amount of variegated pink/purple silk blend yarn

Charms – 1 small face, 1 arm, 1 hand, 2 feet, 3 shoes, 1 handbag, 1 crown

Purple polyester thread and sewing needle

Felt flowers and embossed spirals

3 mm amethyst-coloured glass beads

8 mm pale purple lustre shell cubes

8 mm purple porcelain disc beads

Purple or pink Maria George glass beads

Beading needle

Polyester fibre filling

Wool needle

Using 4.5mm knitting needles and 2 strands of purple yarn, cast on 46 sts.

Row 1: K1, p1, *k2, p2, rep from * to last 2 sts, p1, k1.

Row 2: *K2, p2, rep from * to end.

These 2 rows form rib pattern.

Continue in rib pattern until work measures 17 cm from cast-on edge.

Shape Top

Row 1: K1, p1, *k2, p2tog, rep from * to last 4 sts, k2, p1, k1.

Row 2: K2, *p2, k1 rep from * to last 4 sts, p2, k2.

Row 3: K1, p1, *k2tog, p1, rep from * to last st, k1.

Row 4: K2, p1, *k1, p1, rep from * to last 2 sts, k2.

Row 5: *Sl1, k1, psso, rep from * to last st, k1.

Row 6: K1, purl to last st, k1.

Row 7: K1, k2tog to last st, k1 (7 sts).

Row 8: As row 6.

Row 9: K1, k2tog 3 times.

Break off yarn, thread through rem sts, pull up tightly and fasten off.

Make 2.

To Make Up The Cosy With right sides together, and starting from top centre, stitch the top closed for 5 cm down each side. Stitch up from the lower edge for 4 cm leaving an opening for the handle and the spout. Turn right side out.

MYSTIC MEG

Using 2.75 mm knitting needles and variegated pink/purple yarn, cast on 12 sts.

Row 1: Knit

Row 2: P10, wrap.

Row 3: K8, wrap.

Row 4: P6, wrap.

Row 5: K4, wrap.

Row 6: Purl.

Repeat these 6 rows another 4 times. Cast off.

To Make Up Mystic Meg With right sides together, sew side seam halfway. Turn right side out and stuff firmly. Sew the rest of the seam and then run a gathering thread around the cast-on edge. Pull up firmly and fasten off. Do the same with the other end. Make sure you have sufficient filling and have made a firm, round ball.

Personalizing Meg

Thread a sewing needle with polyester thread. Attach the face charm to the ball by bringing the thread through the hole in the face and then through a glass bead to secure. Go back down through the hole and repeat on the other side. Repeat this several times to ensure that the piece is really secure.

Place the crown above the face and secure in the same manner with 2 beads through the holes. Add the arm in the same way. Make a second arm by stringing some beads onto a length of sewing thread and then adding the hand charm to the end. Stitch firmly in position.

The legs are made in the same way as the beaded hand. Thread a small bead on the needle after attaching the foot and run the needle back through the bead and into the body to secure it. Secure Meg's body to the centre top of the tea cosy with a double length of polyester thread,reinforcing the stitching as necessary.

To Attach Felt Flowers and Beads

Attach 2 felt flowers and spirals to each side of the tea cosy.

Attach the remainder of the porcelain and lustre shell beads to the tea cosy with the polyester thread and the beading needle. Use a 3 mm glass amethyst on top of each bead to secure it. This way the thread does not show at all. Keep turning the cosy round as you sew the beads on so that you get an even distribution. Ensure the beads are securely attached.

Sew the lucky shoe charms and handbag on randomly around the tea cosy.

Peppermint Rock

This cosy is a fabulous project for knitters who want instant results with maximum drama. The basic cosy is made with a knit and purl rib pattern and is suitable for a beginner. The felt batons in complementary colours are randomly applied over the body of the cosy and are held in place with a few easy stitches. A decorative I-cord top knot provides the finishing touch. .

SIZE
To fit a 6-cup teapot

MATERIALS
4 x 50 g balls of aqua DK (8-ply) wool
1 pair 4.5 mm knitting needles
2 x 4 mm double-pointed knitting needles
Wool needle
40 felt batons in green and blue
Polyester thread
Sewing needle

Make 2.

Using 4.5 mm knitting needles and 2 strands of yarn, cast on 46 sts.

Row 1: K1, p1, *k2, p2, rep from * to last 2 sts, p1, k1.

Row 2: *K2, p2, rep from * to end.

These 2 rows form rib pattern.

Continue in rib pattern until work measures 17 cm from cast-on edge.

Shape Top

Row 1: K1, p1, *k2, p2tog, rep from * to last 4 sts, k2, p1, k1.

Row 2: K2, *p2, k1 rep from * to last 4 sts, p2, k2.

Row 3: K1, p1, *k2tog, p1, rep from * to last st, k1.

Row 4: K2, p1, *k1, p1, rep from * to last 2 sts, k2.

Row 5: *Sl1, k1, psso, rep from * to last st, k1.

Row 6: K1, purl to last st, k1.

Row 7: K1, k2tog to last st, k1 (7 sts).

Row 8: As row 6.

Row 9: K1, k2tog 3 times.

Break off yarn, thread through rem sts, pull up tightly and fasten off.

I-CORD LOOP

Using 4 mm double-pointed knitting needles and 2 strands of yarn, cast on 3 sts. Knit one row, do not turn, *slide sts to other end of needle and pull yarn firmly behind, knit next row. Repeat from * until cord is 10 cm long. Slip first st, k2tog, psso, fasten off.

To Make Up Fold the I-cord in half to make a loop. Stitch the ends together, then sew the loop to the top of the cosy.

To Make Up The Tea Cosy With right sides together, stitch the top of the cosy closed for 5 cm down each side. Stitch up from the lower edge for 4 cm leaving an opening for the handle and the spout. Turn right side out.

Put the cosy on the teapot so that it is slightly stretched. This gives a better work surface. Pin the felt batons to the cosy in a random manner. Once you are happy with the look, sew in place using polyester thread and a sewing needle. Take a few stitches to secure the thread to the underside of the cosy, then bring the needle through the baton, and in again in almost the same place for an almost invisible stitch.

Pomp and Circumstance

Made to celebrate the Queen's Diamond Jubilee, this patriotic confection in red, white and blue makes a strong statement and is a fun piece to make. The knitted pompom decorations make an extrovert statement that's perfect for a festival or celebration. The cosy is knitted 'in the round' on a set of double-pointed knitting needles so there are no unsightly seams.

SIZE
To fit a 6-cup teapot

MATERIALS
3 x 50 g balls of red DK (8-ply) wool
1 x 50 g ball of royal blue DK (8-ply) wool
1 x 50 g ball of white DK (8-ply) wool
5 x 4 mm double-pointed knitting needles
2 x 2.75 mm double-pointed knitting needles
Polyester fibre filling
Wool needle

Using 3 x 4 mm double-pointed knitting needles and red DK (8-ply) yarn, cast on 90 sts (30, 30, 30). Join into a ring being careful not to twist the stitches.

Work 5 rounds st st (every round knit).

Picot round: *Yfwd, k2tog, rep from * to end of round.

Work another 5 rounds st st.

Round 12: Fold hem at picot round and knit one stitch together with one loop from cast-on edge until all stitches have been worked.

Work another 5 cm in st st.

Divide for Spout and Handle Openings

Next round: (Place stitch marker.) Knit first 45 sts on to 1 needles. (These will become the first side. Knit the remaining 45 sts onto another needle. You will now be knitting backwards and forwards in rows on the first 45 sts.) Turn.

Next row: K4, purl to last 4 sts, k4.

Next row: Knit.

Rep the last 2 rows until work measures 16 cm from cast-on edge. Break off yarn.

Rejoin yarn and work other side to match, keeping garter stitch border correct.

Once both sides are complete, redistribute stitches evenly back onto three needles ensuring that round starts with stitch marker.

Shape Top

Round 1: *K7, k2 tog, rep from * to end.

Round 2 and even rounds: Knit.

Round 3: *K6, k2tog, rep from * to end.

Round 5: * K5, k2tog, rep from * to end.

Keeping pattern of decreases, continue in this manner until the round k1, k2tog has been worked. Break off yarn. Thread through rem sts, pull up tight and fasten off.

Darn in all loose ends.

KNITTED POMPOMS

Using 3 mm knitting needles and DK (8-ply) yarn, cast on 12 sts.

Row 1: Knit

Row 2: P10, wrap.

Row 3: K8, wrap.

Row 4: P6, wrap.

Row 5: K4, wrap.

Row 6: Purl.

Repeat these 6 rows another 4 times. Cast off. With right sides together, sew side seam half way. Turn right side out and stuff firmly. Sew the rest of the seam and then run a gathering thread around the cast-on edge. Pull up firmly and fasten off. Do the same with the other end. Make sure there is sufficient filling and each is a round, firm ball. Make 24 balls, 8 in each colour.

Starting at the top of the cosy and working out and down, firmly sew on the pompoms. It is easier to do this with the cosy on the teapot as it provides a firm surface on which to work.

Pink Sugar Mice

Who could resist these dear little mice in all their various hues of pink dashing about all over this hot pink tea cosy? Topped by tiny Swarovski crystal beads on their noses and tails, the mice are knitted in oddments of 4-ply yarn and stuffed with polyester fibre filling. Knit as many or as few mice as you like but more is definitely better. The tea cosy can be knitted in 8- or 12-ply yarn and features an attractive textured blackberry stitch pattern.

SIZE
To fit a 6-cup teapot

MATERIALS
2 x 50 g balls of cerise chunky (12-ply) or DK (8-ply) wool
Oddments of 4-ply wool in shades of pink and purple
1 pair 4 mm knitting needles
1 pair 2 mm knitting needles
2 x 2.25 mm double-pointed knitting needles
Polyester fibre filling
Sewing needle
Polyester thread
Swarovski 5 mm crystal beads in black
Swarovski 8 mm crystal beads in pink
Black stranded embroidery cotton
Wool needle

Note DK (8-ply) instructions are given in brackets.

Using 4 mm knitting needles and cerise yarn, cast on 46 sts (chunky/12-ply) or 54 sts (dk/ 8-ply).

Commencing with a knit row, work 6 (8) rows st st.

Picot edge row: K1, *yfwd, k2tog, rep from * to last
2 sts, k2.

Commencing with a purl row, work 7 (9) rows st st.

Next row: Wth right side facing, fold up hem at picot edge row and knit 1 st together with 1 loop from cast-on edge until all sts have been worked off.

Commence Pattern

Row 1: Knit.

Row 2 and all even rows: Purl.

Row 3: P1, *k, p, k all into same st, p3tog, rep from * to last st, p1.

Row 5: P1, *p3tog, k, p, k all into same st, rep from * to last st, p1.

Row 6: Purl.

These 5 rows form pattern.

Continue in patt until work measures 17 cm from picot edge row ending with a row 6.

Commence Decrease

Next row: P1, *p1, p3tog, rep from * to end.

Next row: K2tog all across.

Break off yarn thread through rem sts. Pull up tightly and fasten off.

Make 2.

To Make Up The Cosy With right sides together, stitch the top seam closed working out from the centre point to 5–6 cm down each side. Turn right side out.

Handle and Spout Openings

Using 4 mm knitting needles, cerise 12-ply (8-ply) wool, and with rs facing, pick up and knit 48 (55) sts along one side of the handle opening. Work 12 rows st st. Cast off. Repeat on the other side of the handle opening and then on each side of the spout opening.

To Make Up Fold each piece in half to the wrong side and stitch in place.

Join the bottom seam of the tea cosy at each side for 3–4 cm.

Darn in any loose ends.

PINK SUGAR MICE

Using 2 mm knitting needles and pink 4-ply yarn, cast on 7 sts. Begin with a knit row, work 2 rows st st.

Row 3: K2, inc into next 2 sts, k3.

Row 4 and all even rows: Purl.

Row 5: K3, inc into next 2 sts, k4.

Row 7: K4, inc into next 2 sts, k5.

Continue increasing in the centre 2 sts in this manner until there are 31 sts.

Work 3 rows st st without further shaping.

Next row: K1, (sl1, k1, psso) 7 times, k1, (k2tog) 7 times, k1.

Next row: K1, (sl1, k1, psso) 3 times, k3, (k2tog) 3 times, k1 (11 sts).

Next row: Purl.

Break off yarn, thread through rem sts, pull up tightly and fasten off.

Ears

Using 2 mm knitting needles and pink 4-ply yarn, cast on 3 sts.

Row 1: Inc in first st, k2.
Row 2: Inc in first st, purl to end.
Row 3: Inc in first st, knit to end.
Row 4: Inc in first st, purl to end.
Row 5: Knit.

Break off yarn, thread through rem sts, pull up tightly and fasten off. This is the base of the ear. Make 2.

To Make Up Body With right sides together, fold mouse body in half and stitch seam part-way closed. Turn right side out and stuff firmly. Stitch up the rest of the seam, which forms the underside of the mouse body.
Position the ears on each side of the head, pin in place and then stitch firmly to secure.

Tail

Using 2, 2.25mm double-pointed knitting needles and 4-ply yarn make a 2-stitch I-cord 9–10 cm long. Fasten off. Attach securely to the mouse. Sew a pink 8 mm Swarovski crystal bead to the end of the tail.

Nose and Eyes

Using polyester thread, sew the jet Swarovksi crystal to the nose.
Use two strands of black embroidery cotton and make French knots for the eyes.

Primavera

This tea cosy has an uplifting, spring-like optimism with its cluster of brightly coloured green and blue leaves and fabulous bright green I-cord flower on the top. The centres of the ribbed panels are enhanced with a line of embroidered chain stitch in two contrasting shades of green.

SIZE
To fit a 6-cup teapot

MATERIALS
4 x 50 g ball of cream DK (8-ply) wool
Small amounts of four shades of blue, aqua and bright green DK (8-ply)
1 cm felt ball or button
Crewel embroidery wool in light and dark green
Crewel embroidery needle
1 pair 4.5 mm knitting needles
2 x 2.75mm double-pointed knitting needles
Wool needle

Using 4.5mm knitting needles and two strands of cream DK (8-ply), cast on 46 sts.

Row 1: K1, p1, *k2, p2, rep from * to last 2 sts, p1, k1.

Row 2: *K2, p2, rep from * to end.

These 2 rows form rib pattern.

Continue in rib pattern until work measures 17 cm from cast-on edge.

Shape Top

Row 1: K1, p1, *k2, p2tog, rep from * to last 4 sts, k2, p1, k1.

Row 2: K2, *p2, k1 rep from * to last 4 sts, p2, k2.

Row 3: K1, p1, *k2tog, p1, rep from * to last st, k1.

Row 4: K2 ,p1, *k1, p1, rep from * to last 2 sts, k2.

Row 5: *Sl1, k1, psso, rep from * to last st, k1.

Row 6: K1, purl to last st, k1.

Row 7: K1, k2tog to last st, k1 (7 sts).

Row 8:As row 6.

Row 9:K1, k2tog 3 times.

Break off yarn, thread through rem sts, pull up tightly and fasten off. Make 2.

Work a row of chain stitch up the centre of each rib panel using crewel embroidery wool, alternating between light and dark green yarn.

To Make Up Cosy With right sides together, stitch the top of the cosy together, working out from the centre and 5 cm down each side. Stitch up from the lower edge for 4 cm leaving an opening for the handle and spout. Turn right side out.

FLOWER

For the central flower make an I-cord using 2.75 mm double-pointed knitting needles and bright green DK (8-ply) yarn to 50 cm long. Fasten off. Fold into 5 even petals, leaving a short length of stem, secure firmly using small stitches, then place the felt ball or button in the centre. Sew securely to the top of the tea cosy.

LEAVES

Make 7 in a shades of blues, aqua and green. Using 2.75 mm double-pointed knitting needles and a shade of blue, green or aqua, cast on 3 sts. Work an I-cord for 1.5 cm.

Row 1: (rs) Knit.

Row 2: Knit.

Row 3: K1, m1, k1, m1, k1.

Row 4 and all even rows: Knit.

Row 5: K2, m1, k1, m1, k2.

Row 7: K3 m1, k1, m1, k3.

Row 9: K4, m1, k1, m1, k4.

Row 11: K5, m1, k1, m1, k5.

Rows 13 and 15: Knit.

Row 17: K5, sl2, k1, psso, k5.

Row 19: K4, sl2, k1, psso, k4.

Row 21: K3, sl2, k1, psso, k3.

Row 23: K2, sl2, k1, psso, k2.

Rows 24 and 26: Purl.

Row 25: K1, sl2, k1, psso, k1 (3 sts).

Row 27: K1, sl2, psso, fasten off.

To Decorate The Cosy Sew leaves evenly around the central flower.

I-CORDS

Using 2.75 mm double-pointed knitting needles and DK (8-ply) green, make 7 I-cords 7–10 cm long. Stitch to the tea cosy.

Purple Patch

Purple lovers, this is one for you. A plain stocking-stitch body in lively violet provides the background for an array of purple knitted patches – as well as the perfect opportunity to use up remnants of your favourite colour. A darker contrast border and decorative I-cords complete the look on this symphony of purple tea cosy.

SIZE
To fit a 6-cup teapot

MATERIALS
1 x 50 g ball of bright purple DK (8-ply) wool
1 x 50 g ball of dark purple DK (8-ply) wool
Small amounts of DK (8-ply) in the following shades: mauve, cream, mid purple, very dark purple
5 x 4 mm double-pointed knitting needles
2 x 2.75 mm double-pointed knitting needles
Wool needle

Using 4 mm double-pointed knitting needles and dark purple DK (8-ply) yarn, cast on 90 sts, (30, 30, 30). Join into a ring, being careful not to twist the stitches.

Work 5 rounds st st (every round knit).

Picot edge round: *Yfwd, k2tog, rep from * to end of round.

Work another 5 rounds st st.

Round 12: Fold hem at picot edge and knit 1 stitch together with 1 loop from cast-on edge until all stitches have been worked. Break off dark purple and join in bright purple.

Work another 5 cm in st st.

Divide for Spout and Handle Openings

Next round: Place stitch marker. Knit 45 sts on to 1 needle for first side. Knit the remaining 45 sts onto a second needles. You will be knitting backwards and forwards in rows on the first 45 sts. Turn.

Next row: K4, purl to last 4 sts, k4.

Next row: Knit.

Rep the last 2 rows until work measures 16 cm from beg. Break off yarn.

Rejoin yarn and work other side to match, keeping garter stitch border correct.

Redistribute stitches evenly back on to three needles for top shaping, ensuring that the round starts with the stitch marker.

Shape Top

Round 1: *K7, k2tog, rep from * to end.

Round 2 and all even rounds: Knit.

Round 3: *K6, k2tog, rep from * to end.

Round 5: *K5, k2tog, rep from * to end.

Keeping continuity of decreases, continue in this manner until the round k1, k2tog has been worked. Break off yarn. Thread through rem sts, pull up tight and fasten off.

Darn in all loose ends.

PATCHES

The patches are made using 2 contrasting shades of yarn. Make 8 using different colour combinations.

Using 4 mm knitting needles and yarn A, cast on 19 sts.

Row 1: K1tbl, k7, k3tog, k7, slip last st wyif.

Row 2 and all even rows: K1tbl, knit to last st, slip last st wyif.

Row 3: K1tbl, k6, k3tog, k6, slip last st wyif.

Row 5: K1tbl, k5, k3tog, k5, slip last st wyif.

Row 7: K1tbl, k4, k3tog, k4, slip last st wyif.

Row 9: K1tbl, k3, k3tog, k3, slip last st wyif.

Row 11: K1tbl, k2, k3tog, k2, slip last st wyif.

Row 13: K1tbl, k1, k3tog, k1, slip last st wyif.

Row 15: K1tbl, k3tog, slip last st wyif.

Row 17: K3tog. Break off yarn, Thread through rem st and fasten off. Darn in ends.

To Decorate Cosy Sew 4 mitred squares to each side of the tea cosy.

I-CORD TOP KNOT

Using 2.75 mm knitting needles and purple DK (8-ply), cast on 3 sts. Knit 1 row. Do not turn. *Slide sts to other end of needle and pull yarn firmly behind work. K3, rep from * until cord is 10 cm long. Sl2, k1, psso. Fasten off. Make 6.

To Make Up Sew the I-cords to the top centre, arranging them evenly around the cosy.

Rainy Days Cabled

A cabled tea cosy somehow seems extra snug and warming, just like a cabled jumper. Cables work best in a single colour, and you can choose from a stylish, restrained cosy, such as the charcoal grey one here, a bright fluorescent one for a big fun factor, or indeed anything in between!

SIZE
To fit a 6-cup teapot

MATERIALS
4 x 50 g balls charcoal grey DK (8-ply) wool
1 pair 4.5 mm knitting needles
Cable needle
2 x 4 mm double-pointed knitting needles
Wool needle

Using 4.5 mm knitting needles and 2 strands of yarn, cast on 42 sts.

Row 1: K1, p1, *k2, p2, rep from * to last 2 sts, p1, k1.

Row 2. *K2, p2, rep from * to end.

Rep these 2 rows twice more (6 rows in total).

CABLE ABBREVIATIONS

CB4: Slip next 2 sts onto cable needle and hold at back of work, k2 and then k2 from cable needle.

Cr3L: Slip next 2 sts onto cable needle and hold at front of work, p1, k2 from cable needle.

Cr3R: Slip next st onto cable needle and hold at back of work, k2, p1 from cable needle.

CABLE PATTERN

Row 1: K1, *p1, Cr3L, Cr3R, p1, rep from * to last st, k1.

Row 2: K3, *p4, k4, rep from * to last 7 sts, p4, k3.

Row 3: K1, *p2, CB4, p2, rep from * to last st, k1.

Row 4: As row 2.

Row 5: K1, *p1, Cr3R, Cr3L, p1, rep from *to last st, k1.

Row 6: *K2, p2, rep from * to last 2 sts, k2.

Work another 6 rows rib as for rows 1 and 2 followed by the cable pattern. Then repeat this 12-row sequence once more. You will now have completed three sets of cable patterns.

Shape Top

Row 1: K1, p1, *k2, p2tog, rep from * to last 4 sts, k2, p1, k1.

Row 2: K2, *p2, k1 rep from * to last 4 sts p2, k2.

Row 3: K1, p1, *k2tog, p1, rep from * to last st, k1.

Row 4: K2, p1, *k1, p1, rep from * to last 2 sts, k2.

Row 5: *Sl1, k1, psso, rep from * to last st, k1.

Row 6: K1, purl to last st, k1.

Row 7: K1, k2tog to last st, k1 (7 sts).

Row 8: As row 6.

Row 9: K1, k2tog 3 times.

Break off yarn, thread through rem sts, pull up tightly and fasten off.

Make 2

I-CORD LOOPS

Using 4 mm double-pointed knitting needles, cast on 3 sts. Knit one row, do not turn, *slide sts to other end of needle and pull yarn firmly behind. Knit next row. Repeat from * until cord is 10 cm long. Sl1, k2tog, psso, fasten off.

Make 3.

Fold the cords in half to create a loop. Stitch firmly closed and then stitch the loop to the top of the cosy. Repeat with the other two loops.

Sea Anemone

This anemone tea cosy is a real source of fascination for small children. It's a little bit like a sea creature found in a rock pool at the seaside with its wavy tentacles. It is not at all difficult to make but looks amazing, especially if you use plenty of different shades of pink for the 'I' Cord tentacles. By not making them more than 5 cm long they will stand upright when the cosy is sitting on the teapot.

SIZE
To fit a 6-cup teapot

MATERIALS
2 x 2.75mm double-pointed
    knitting needles
Partial balls of cream and
    5 shades of pink DK (8-ply)
    wool
4 x 50 g ball of pale pink dk
    (8-ply) wool
1 pair 4.5 mm knitting needles
Wool needle

I-CORD TENTACLES

Using 2.75 mm double-pointed knitting needles and a small ball of wool, cast on 3 sts. Knit 1 row. Do not turn. *Slide sts to other end of needle and pull yarn firmly behind work. K3 sts, rep from * until cord is 5 cm long. Sl2, k1, psso. Transfer remaining st to circular needle and set aside. Make 95 in all shades of pink and cream. Mix the colours as you knit so that when the cords are knitted into the cosy you will have different shades next to each other.

TEA COSY

Using 4.5 mm knitting needles and 2 strands of pink DK (8-ply), cast on 46 sts.

Row 1: K1, p1, *k2, p2, rep from * to last 2 sts, p1, k1.

Row 2: *K2, p2, rep from * to end.

These 2 rows form rib pattern.

Work another 6 rows rib.

Row 9 Adding I-cords: K1, p1, k1,*k1 together with an I-cord, p2, k2, p2, rep from * to last 3 sts, k1, p1, k1.

Work 3 rows rib.

Row 13: K1, p1, k2, p2, k1,*k1 together with an I-cord, p2, k2, p2, rep from * k1, p2, k2, p1, k1.

Repeat the last 5 pattern rows twice more.

Work 3 rows rib.

Row 27: K1, p1, k1, *k1 together with an I-cord, p2, k2, p2, rep from * to last 3 sts, k1, p1, k1.

Shape Top

Row 1: K1, p1, *k2, p2tog, rep from * to last 4 sts, k2, p1, k1.

Row 2: K2, *p2, k1 rep from * to last 4 sts, p2, k2.

Row 3: K1, p1, *k2tog, p1, rep from * to last st, k1.

Row 4: K2, p1, *k1, p1, rep from * to last 2 sts, k2.

Row 5: *Sl1, k1, psso, rep from * to last st, k1.

Row 6: K1, purl to last st, k1.

Row 7: K1, k2tog to last st, k1 (7 sts).

Row 8: As row 6.

Row 9: K1, k2tog 3 times.

Break off yarn, thread through rem sts, pull up tightly and fasten off.

To Make Up Cosy With right sides together, stitch the top closed for 5 cm down each side. Stitch up from the lower edge for 4 cm leaving an opening for the handle and the spout. Turn right side out.

TOP KNOT

Gather together the remaining 11 'I' Cords using a length of yarn threaded through the remaining stitch of each. Secure firmly to the top of the tea cosy fanning out to make an even shape.

Sew in all loose ends.

Silk Roses

This traditional tea cosy design is lifted out of the ordinary by its sumptuous decoration of very fine Kid Silk mohair roses. The shadesof pink and purple endow the cosy with a refined elegance. This is a great project for a novice knitter The only thing to note is that the roses are crocheted with fine mohair, so if you are a beginner it's advisable to practise first with thicker yarn

SIZE
To fit a 6-cup teapot

MATERIALS
2 x 50 g balls of deep pink
    chunky (12-ply) DK or (8-ply)
    wool
1 pair 4 mm knitting needles
Wool needle
Small amount of Rowan Kid
    Silk mohair or other very
    fine mohair in green and
    3 or 4 shades of pink
3 mm crochet hook

Note The instructions for the dk (8-ply) yarn is given in brackets.

Using 4 mm knitting needles cast on 46 sts (chunky/12-ply) or 54 sts (DK/8-ply)
Beginning with a knit row, work 6 (8) rows st st.
Picot edge row: K1, *yfwd, k2tog, rep from * to last 2 sts, k2.
Beginning with a purl row, work another 7 (9) rows st st.
Next row: Wth right side facing, fold up hem at picot row and knit 1 st together with 1 loop from cast-on edge until all sts have been worked.

Commence Pattern
Row 1: Knit.
Row 2 and all even rows: Purl.
Row 3: P1, *k, p, k all into same st, p3tog, rep from * to last st, p1.
Row 5: P1, *p3tog, k, p, k all into same st, rep from * to last st, p1.
Row 6: Purl.
These 5 rows form pattern.
Continue in pattern until work measures 17 cm from picot edge row and ending with a row 6 pattern.
Next row: P1, *p1, p3tog, rep from * to end.
Next row: K2tog all across.
Break off yarn thread through rem sts. Pull up tightly and fasten off.

To Make Up With right sides together, stitch the top seam closed, working from the centre point out and down 5–6 cm on each side. Turn right side out.

Handle and Spout Openings
Using 4 mm knitting needles and chunky/12-ply (DK/8-ply) wool, and with the right side facing, pick up and knit 48 (55) sts along both pieces at each side of the tea cosy. Work 12 rows st st. Cast off.
Make 2.

To Make Up Cosy Fold each piece to the wrong side and stitch in place. Join the bottom seam for 3–4 cm.
Sew in any loose ends.

ROSES
Using 3 mm crochet hook and Kid Silk mohair, make 48ch. Turn, and miss 4ch, dtr into next 43ch, tr into last ch.
Next row: 3ch, 3tr into each dtr, to last 2 sts, 1 dbl, sl into last tr.
Fasten off.
Starting at the end with the sl st and dbl crochet, roll the rose up, securing with small stitches at the base.
Make at least 4.
Attach the roses to the top of the tea cosy with secure stitches.

LEAVES
Using 2.75 mm double-pointed knitting needles and green Kid Silk mohair, cast on 3 sts. Work an I-cord for 1.5 cm.
Row 1: (rs) Knit.
Row 2: Purl.
Row 3: K1, m1, k1, m1, k1.
Row 4 and all even rows: K1, purl to last st, k1.
Row 5: K2, m1, k1, m1, k2.

Row 7: K3 m1, k1, m1, k3.
Row 9: K4, m1, k1, m1, k4.
Row 11: K5, m1, k1, m1, k5.
Rows 13 and 15: Knit.
Row 17: K5, sl2, k1, psso, k5.
Row 19: K4, sl2, k1, psso, k4.
Row 21: K3, sl2, k1, psso, k3.
Row 23: K2, sl2, k1,psso, k2.
Rows 24 and 26: Purl.
Row 25: K1, sl2, k1, psso, k1 (3 sts).
Row 27: K1, sl2, psso, fasten off.
Make 5–6.

To Decorate The Cosy Sew leaves among the roses making sure they are evenly spread out.

Sunset Cables

Sometimes a beautiful yarn does not need much in the way of fancy pattern or decoration; and this beautiful variegated Noro Iro yarn is one of them. Knitted with a plain ground and decorated with a few bold cables, it shows the rich combination of colours to perfection. Two dramatic top knots provide a final flourish.

SIZE
To fit a 6-cup teapot

MATERIALS
1 x 100 g ball of Noro Iro
1 pair 5 mm knitting needles
Cable needle
Wool needle
Polyester fibre filling

CABLE ABBREVIATIONS

T5BP: Slip next 3 sts onto cable needle and hold at back of work, k2 from left-hand needle, p1 from cable needle and knit rem 2 from cable needle.

T3B: Slip next st on to cable needle and hold at back of work, knit next 2 sts from left-hand needle, then purl st from cable needle.

T3F: Slip next 2 sts onto cable needle and hold at front of work. P1 from left-hand needle, then knit 2 from cable needle.

TEA COSY

Using 5 mm knitting needles and Noro Iro, cast on 48 sts. Work 4 rows garter st (every row knit).
Row 1: P5, T5BP, p12, T5BP, p12, T5BP, p4.
Row 2 and all even rows: Knit all knit sts and purl all purl sts as they appear.
Row 3: P4, *T3B, p1, T3F, p10, rep from * to last 3 sts, p3.
Row 5: P3, *T3B, p3, T3F, p8, rep from * to last 2 sts, p2.
Row 7: P3,* k2, p5, k2, p8, rep from * to last 2 sts, p2.
Row 9: P4, *T3F, p3, T3B, p8, rep from * to last 2 sts, p2.
Row 11: P4, *T3F, p1, T3B, p10, rep from * to last 3 sts, p3.
Row 12: As row 2.
These 12 rows form pattern.
Work 2 more pattern repeats.

Shape Top

Dec row: P5, *T5BP, p2tog 6 times, rep from * to last 4 sts, p4.
Row 2: K2tog twice, *p2tog, p1, p2tog, k2tog 3 times rep from * to last 5 sts, k2tog twice, k1.
Row 3: Sl1, p2tog, psso, * sl1, k2tog, psso, p2tog, rep from * to last 3 sts, sl1, k2tog psso.
Break off yarn, thread trough rem sts, pull up tightly and fasten off.
Make 2.

To Make Up It may be easier to sew up the tea cosy using finer yarn in the same colour. With right sides together and starting at centre top, sew the seams together to 4 cm down each side. Sew the lower edges together for 3 cm leaving openings for the handle and the spout. Darn in all loose ends.

SMALL KNITTED BALL

Using 5 mm knitting needles and Noro Iro, cast on 12 sts.
Row 1: Knit.
Row 2: P10, wrap.
Row 3: K8, wrap.
Row 4: P6, wrap.
Row 5: K4, wrap.
Row 6: Purl.
Rep these 6 rows another 4 times. Cast off.
With right sides together, sew side seam halfway. Turn right side out and stuff firmly. Sew the rest of the seam, then run a gathering thread around the cast-on edge. Pull up firmly and fasten off. Do the same with the other end. Stuff firmly. Stitch the balls securely to the top of the cosy.

Note It is easier to do this with the cosy on the teapot as it provides a firm surface on which to work.

LARGE KNITTED BALL

Make as for the small knitted ball, but cast on 16 sts.

Make the first turning row with 14 sts, and the last turning row with 8 sts.

Complete 6 repeats of the 6 rows instead of 5.

Complete in the same way.

Tangerine Dreams

This cabled tea cosy has a bright tangerine glow and is textured all over. The simple cable pattern makes the knitted fabric much bulkier and therefore warmer. This is a superb way to practise a stitch like cable that you might avoid for a larger-scale project, and then you'll have the confidence to use the stitch again. Three knitted balls add neat top decoration.

SIZE
To fit a 6-cup teapot

MATERIALS
1 pair 4 mm knitting needles
1 x 50 g ball pink DK (8-ply) wool
1 x 50 g ball dark orange dk (8-ply) wool
2 x 50 g balls orange dk (8-ply) wool
2 x 2.75 mm double-pointed knitting needles
Cable needle
Wool needle
Polyester fibre filling

CABLE ABBREVIATION

4RC: Sl next 2 sts onto cable needle and hold at back of work, k2, then k2 from cable needle.

Using 4 mm knitting needles and pink, cast on 45 sts. Beginning with a knit row, work in st st for 10 rows.

Fold 5 rows of hem to the inside and knit 1 st together with 1 loop from cast-on edge. Cont in this manner until all sts have been worked.

Row 11: Purl.

Change to dark orange.

Row 12: K2, m1 (7 times), k4, m1 (3 times), k2, m1 (7 times) (62 sts).

Row 13: Purl.

Break off dark orange and join in orange.

CABLE PATTERN

Rows 1 and 3: (rs) Knit.

Row 2: Purl.

Row 4: *K2, p4 rep from * to end.

Row 5: P2, *4RC, p2, rep from * to end.

Row 6: Purl

Work in cable pattern until work measures 16 cm ending with a row 6.

Shape Top

Work in stripes of 2 rows orange, 2 rows dark orange, 2 rows pink.

Next row: *K1, k2tog, rep from * to last 2 sts, k2tog.

Next row: Purl.

Next row: *K1, k2tog, rep from * to last 2 sts, k2tog.

Next row: Purl.

Next row: *K1, k2tog, rep from * to end.

Next row: *K1, k2tog, rep from * to end.

Break off yarn, thread through rem sts, pull up tightly and fasten off.

Make 2.

To Make Up Join pieces together at the top for 3 cm at each side of the centrepoint.

Spout and Handle Openings

Using 4 mm knitting needles and pink, and with right sides facing, pick up and knit 76 sts along one side.

Working in st st, work 4 rows pink, 2 rows dark orange, 2 rows pink, 2 rows dark orange and 2 rows pink. Cast off.

Fold hem in half and sl st neatly to the inside. Work the other sides to match.

KNITTED BALLS

Using 2.75 mm double-pointed knitting needles and yarn, cast on 12 sts.

Row 1: Knit.

Row 2: P10, wrap.

Row 3: K8, wrap.

Row 4: P6, wrap.

Row 5: K4, wrap.

Row 6: Purl.

Rep these 6 rows another 4 times. Cast off.

With right sides together, sew side seam half way. Turn right side out and stuff firmly. Sew the rest of the seam and then run a gathering thread around the cast-on edge. Pull up firmly and fasten off. Do the same with the other end. Making sure you have a round firm ball.

Make 3 balls; 1 in each colour.

Stitch the balls firmly to the top of the cosy.

The Bees Knees

Large, velvety bumble bees hovering around
nectar-laden petals in a summer garden
in the sunshine were the inspiration for
this playful tea cosy. Knit it up using bold,
summery colours for an excessive, jamboree
statement that is sure to get people talking.

SIZE
To fit a 6-cup teapot

MATERIALS
Small amount of cream DK
    (8-ply) wool
1 pair of 4 mm knitting needles
2 x 50 g ball yellow DK (8-ply)
    wool
2 x 50 g balls orange DK (8-ply)
    wool
Small amount of 4 ply in black,
    yellow and white
Oddments of pink and green
    DK (8-ply) wool
Polyester fibre filling
4 x 2 mm double-pointed
    knitting needles
2 x 2.75 mm double-pointed
    knitting needles
3 mm crochet hook
Wool needle

Note The pleated fabric is created pulling the yarn not in use tightly across on the wrong side. It is important to do this on each row. Carry the yarn on the back of the work and right to the ends. It may seem a little slow to begin with, but you will develop a rhythm.

Using 4 mm knitting needles and cream DK (8-ply) yarn, cast on 98 sts. Work 8 rows garter st (every row knit). Remove cream and fasten in orange (A) and yellow (B).
Row 1: K1A, k6B, *k7A, k7B, rep from * to last 7 sts. k6A, k1B. As you knit, pull the yarn not in use very firmly behind, to draw up the pleats.
Row 2: K1B, k6A, *k7B, k6A, rep from * to last 7 sts, k6B, k1A. Keep yarn to the front in this row and continue to pull the yarn not in use tightly so that pleat remains firm.
These 2 rows form pattern. Continue in pattern until 48 rows have been worked.
Commence Decreases rs facing
Row 1: K2togA, k3B, k2togB, *k2togA, k3A, k2togB, k3B, k2togB, rep from * to last 7 sts, k2togA, k3A, k2togB.
Row 2: K1B, k4A, *k5B, k5A, rep from * to last 5 sts, k4B, k1A.
Row 3: K2togA, k1B, k2togB, *k2togA, k1A, k2togA, k2togB, k1B, k2togB rep from * to last 5 sts, k2togA, k1A, k2togB.
Row 4: K1B, k2A, *k3B, k3A, rep from * to last 3 sts, k2B, k1A.
Row 5: K2togA, k1B, *k2togA, k1B, k2togB, k1B, rep from * to last 3 sts, k2togA, k1B.
Row 6: K1B, k1A, *k2B, k2A, rep from * to last 2 sts, k1B, k1A.
Row 7: (K2togA) twice, *k2togB, k2togA, rep from

* to last 4 sts, (k2togB) twice.
Break off yarn, thread through rem sts, pull up tightly and fasten off.
Make 2.

To Make Up Darn in any loose ends. With right sides together, stitch from the centre top down each side for 5 cm. Join sides together at the bottom edge, stitching up each side for 3–4 cm. Turn right side out.

BEE
Using double-pointed knitting needles and black 4-ply yarn, cast on 6 sts on 3 needles (2, 2, 2). Join into a ring, being careful not to twist sts. Knit one round.
Round 2: Inc in every st (12 sts).
Round 3: Knit.
Round 4: Inc in every st (24 sts).
Round 5: Knit.
Round 6: On each needle k6, k2tog.
Round 7: Knit.
Round 8: K2, k2tog, k5, k2tog, k5, k2tog, k3.
Round 9: Knit.
Round 10: *K1, k2tog, rep from * to end.
Round 11: Knit.
Join in yellow 4-ply yarn.
Round 12: Inc in every st (24 sts).
Round 13: Knit.
Round 14: K1, inc in next st, k8, inc in next st, k2, inc in next st, k8, inc in next st, k1.
Round 15: Knit.
Change to black 4-ply yarn.
Work 3 rounds black st st without further shaping.
Change to yellow 4-ply yarn.

Round 19: K1, k2tog, k10, k2tog, k2, k2tog, k10, k2tog, k1.
Round 20: Knit.
Round 21: K1, k2tog, k8, k2tog, k2, k2tog, k8, k2tog, k1.
Round 22: Knit.
Change to black 4-ply yarn.
Round 24: *K2, k2tog, rep from * to end.
Round 25: Knit.
Round 26: *K1, k2tog, rep from * to end.
Fill bee very firmly with polyester fibre filling.
Round 27: K2tog (6 times).
Round 28: K2tog (3 times), break off yarn, thread through rem sts, pull up tightly and fasten off.
Make 3.

Wings

Using 2 mm knitting needles and white 4-ply yarn, cast on 3 sts.
Knit 1 row, then continue in garter st.
Row 2: Inc at each end of row (5 sts).
Row 3: Inc at each end of row (7 sts).
Row 4: Knit.
Row 5: Inc at each end of row.
Work 3 rows without further shaping.
Row 9: Sl1, k1, psso, knit to last 2 sts, k2tog.
Row 10: Knit.
Row 11: Sl1, k1, psso, knit to last 2 sts, k2tog.
Row 12: Sl1, k1, psso, knit to last 2 sts, k2tog.
Cast off.
Make 2 for each bee.

To Make Up Stitch the bees' wings to the centre of the back using the cast-off row as the base of the wing.
Make the antennae by drawing a length of black yarn through the top of the head and knotting the end. Take a small stitch of white yarn through the side of the head to form the eyes.

SINGLE DAISIES

Using 3 mm crochet hook and desired colour of DK (8-ply) yarn make 6ch, form into a loop with a sl st.
Work 1ch, then 11dc into the loop formed. Sl st into first dc.
Break off first colour and join in contrast colour.
Make *11ch, sl st into next dc, rep from * until 12 petals have been completed. Fasten off.

DOUBLE DAISIES

These are similar to the single daisies with an additional row of petals worked into the front loops of the dc.
Using 3 mm crochet hook and desired colour of dk (8-ply) yarn make 6ch. Form into a loop with a sl st.
Work 1ch, then 11dc into the loop formed.
Sl st into first dc. Break off first colour and join in contrast.
*Work 1ch, sl st into front loop of next dc, 1ch, 1dc, 2tr, 1dc into front loop of next dc, rep from * to end with sl st to complete. Break off colour and join in second contast. Working into the back loops of dc round.
*12 ch, sl st into next dc, rep from * until 12 petals have been completed. Fasten off.

LEAVES

Using 2.75 mm double-pointed knitting needles and green DK (8-ply) yarn cast on 3 sts. Work an I-cord for 1.5 cm.
Row 1: (rs) Knit.

Row 2: Purl.

Row 3: K1, m1, k1, m1, k1.

Row 4 and all even rows: K1 purl to last st, k1.

Row 5: K2, m1, k1, m1, k2.

Row 7: K3 m1, k1, m1, k3.

Row 9: K4, m1, k1, m1, k4.

Row 11: K5, m1, k1, m1, k5.

Rows 13 and 15: Knit.

Row 17: K5, sl2, k1, psso, k5.

Row 19: K4, sl2, k1, psso, k4.

Row 21: k3, sl2, k1, psso, k3.

Row 23: K2, sl2, k1, psso, k2.

Rows 24 and 26: Purl.

Row 25: K1, sl2, k1, psso, k1 (3 sts).

Row 27: K1, sl2, psso, fasten off.

Make 4.

To Make Up Sew in all ends. It is easier to attach the bees, flowers and leaves to the cosy when it is on the teapot. Centre the leaves so that they radiate out from the top of the tea cosy. Pin on the flowers. Finally, position the bees. When you are happy with the arrangement stitch each in place.

Tea and Cupcakes

Cupcakes have caught the public imagination and have become a popular design motif. This teacosy takes the motif to a whole new level with 3-dimensional large-as-life knitted cupcakes stitched to the body of the tea cosy. Make as many or as few as you like and experiment with the colours. Leave the cherry off the top of some and embroider hundreds and thousands or sew tiny sparkly beads on others. The possibilities are endless. Let your imagination run wild.

SIZE
To fit a 6-cup teapot

MATERIALS
1 pair of 4.5 mm knitting needles
4 x 50 g balls bright pink DK (8-ply) wool.
1 x 50 g ball cream 4-ply cotton
Small amounts of 4-ply wool in orange, pink, pale pink, yellow
1 pair of 2 mm knitting needles
1 pair of 2.25 mm knitting needles
2 x 2.25 mm double-pointed knitting needles
Polyester fibre filling
Wool needle

Using 4.5 mm knitting needles and 2 strands of bright pink DK (8-ply) yarn, cast on 46 sts.
Row 1: K1, p1, *k2, p2, rep from * to last 2 sts, p1, k1.
Row 2. *K2, p2, rep from * to end.
These 2 rows form rib pattern.
Continue in rib pattern until work measures 17 cm from cast-on edge.

Shape Top

Row 1: K1, p1, *k2, p2tog, rep from * to last 4 sts, k2, p1, k1.
Row 2: K2, *p2, k1 rep from * to last 4 sts, p2, k2.
Row 3: K1, p1, *k2tog, p1, rep from * to last st, k1.
Row 4: K2, p1, *k1, p1, rep from * to last 2 sts, k2.
Row 5: *Sl1, k1, psso, rep from * to last st, k1.
Row 6: K1, purl to last st, k1.
Row 7: K1, k2tog to last st, k1 (7 sts).
Row 8: As row 6.
Row 9: K1, k2tog 3 times.
Break off yarn, thread through rem sts, pull up tightly and fasten off.
Make 2.

To Make Up Cosy With right sides together, stitch the top closed for 5 cm down each side. Stitch up from the lower edge for 4 cm leaving an opening for the handle and the spout. Turn right side out.

CUPCAKES

Using 2 mm knitting needles and cream 4-ply yarn, cast on 12 sts.
Row 1: Purl.
Row 2: Inc in every st.
Row 3: Purl.

Row 4: *Inc, k1, rep from * to last st, k1.
Row 5: Purl.
Row 6: *Inc, k2, rep from * to last 2 sts, k2 (48 sts).
Row 7: Purl.
Row 8: Purl.
Work 6 rows k1, p1 rib.
Change to 2.25 mm knitting needles. Work another 6 rows k1, p1 rib. Break off cream and join in chosen 4-ply colour for top.
St st 2 rows.
Dec row: *K4, k2tog, rep from * to end.
Work 3 rows st st, beg with a purl row.
Dec row: *K3, k2tog, rep from * to end.
Work 3 rows st st, beg with a purl row
Dec row: *K2, k2tog, rep from * to end.
Purl 1 row.
Dec row: *K1, k2tog, rep from * to end.
Purl 1 row.
Dec row: * K2tog, rep from * to end.
Purl 1 row.
Break off yarn, thread through rem sts, pull up tightly and fasten off.
Make at least 5, varying the colours.

Cherry

Using two 2.25 mm double-pointed knitting needles and red 4-ply wool, cast on 1 st.
K, p, k, p, k into same st (5 sts).
Row 1: Purl.
Row 2: Knit.
Row 3: Purl.
Row 4: Knit.
Row 5: Purl.
Row 6: Knit, pass, *second st on right-hand needle over the first st, rep from * until 1 st rem.

Fasten off. Make 1 for each cupcake.
Run a gathering stitch around the outside of the
cherry. Draw up to form a rounded shape. Fasten
off and stitch to the top of the cupcake.

To Make Up With right sides together, stitch
top side seam closed. Gather cast-on edge and
pull up tightly. Sew side seam partially closed
and then turn right side out. Stuff firmly with
polyester fibre filling. Stitch side seam closed.
Attach one cake to the top centre of the tea cosy
and the remainder randomly around the sides of
the cosy.

Patchwork Cosy

Hexagons are a traditional shape used in patchwork quilts, and this delightful design would make a fabulous present for a patchworking enthusiast. Knit the hexagons in oddments of toning colours and apply them to the surface of the cosy so that they look like patchwork pieces.

SIZE
To fit a 6-cup teapot

MATERIALS
2 x 50 g balls of royal blue DK
   (8-ply) wool
1 x 50 g ball of navy blueDK
   (8-ply) wool
Small amounts of 4-ply wool in
   4 or 5 shades of blue
3 x 2.25 mm double-pointed
   knitting needles
5 x 4 mm double-pointed
   knitting needles
Wool needle

Using 4 mm double-pointed knitting needles and navy blue DK (8-ply), cast on 90 sts (30, 30, 30). Join into a ring, being careful not to twist the stitches.

Work 5 rounds st st (every round knit).

Picot round: *Yfwd, k2tog, rep from * to end of round.

Work another 5 rounds st st.

Round 12: Fold a hem at the picot round and knit one stitch off the needle together with one loop from the cast-on edge until all stitches have been worked.

Change to royal blue. Work another 5 cm in st st.

Divide for Spout and Handle Openings

Next round: Place stitch marker. Knit first 45 sts on to 1 needle. These will become the first side. Knit the remaining 45 sts onto another needle. You will now be knitting backwards and forwards in rows on the first 45 sts. Turn.

Next row: K4, purl to last 4 sts, k4.

Next Row: Knit.

Rep the last 2 rows until work measures 16 cm from beg. Break off yarn.

Rejoin yarn and work other side to match, keeping garter stitch border correct.

Once both sides are complete, redistribute stitches evenly onto three needles ready to commence top shaping. Ensure the round starts with the stitch marker.

Shape Top

Round 1: *K7, k2tog, rep from * to end.

Round 2 and all even rounds: Knit.

Round 3: *K6, k2tog, rep from * to end.

Round 5: *K5, k2tog, rep from * to end.

Keeping pattern of decreases, continue in this manner until the round k1, k2tog has been worked. Break off yarn. Thread through rem sts, pull up tight and fasten off.

To Make Up Sew in all loose ends.

PATCHWORK HEXAGONS

Using two 2.25 mm double-pointed knitting needles and shade of blue 4-ply, cast on 20 sts. Have the needle holding the stitches in your left hand and 2 empty needles side by side in your right hand. *Slip the first st purlwise onto the needle closest to you. Slip the second st back on to the needle, rep from * until all sts are on 2 needles. You will have 10 on each. The knitting is now worked backwards and forwards in rows with increases at the sides.

Row 1: Inc in first st, knit to last 2 sts, inc in next sts, k1. Turn work and repeat with sts on the second needle.

Row 2: Knit.

Repeat rows 1 and 2 until you have 40 sts: 20 per needle.

Commence Decrease

Row 1: Sl1, k1, psso, knit to last 2 sts, k2tog. Repeat with sts on other needle.

Row 2: Knit.

Repeat these 2 rows until you have 10 sts left on each needle.

Cast off. Make 8.

To Make Up The Patchwork Join 4 hexagons together and sew to each side of the tea cosy. Darn in all loose ends.

SMALL PATCHWORK HEXAGONS

Work in the same way as for large patchwork hexagons but cast on 6 sts and increase to 12 sts. Decrease again to 6 sts.

Make 7.

Sew six small hexagons around one hexagon to make a single patch. Centre the patch over the top of the tea cosy. Pin in place, then stitch all round the edge.

The Little Caterpillar

This cute little caterpillar tea cosy is bound to be a hit with small people. The body of the little beastie is made using knitted balls arranged in alternating colourways in a sinuous shape on top of the cosy. His head is made o a slightly larger knitted ball and is complete with smiley face. The thick cosy beneath is knitted with blackberry stitch and is not difficult to make.

SIZE
To fit a 6-cup teapot

MATERIALS
2 x 50 g balls of chunky (12-ply) or dk (8-ply) orange wool
Small amounts of DK (8-ply) wool in red, bright green, yellow, bright blue, brown, lime green and olive green
1 pair of 4 mm knitting needles
2 x 2.75 mm double-pointed knitting needles
Polyester fibre filling
Stranded embroidery cotton in yellow and green
Sewing needle
Wool needle

Note DK (8-ply) version is given in brackets.
Using 4 mm knitting needles and orange, cast on
46 sts (12-ply) or 54 sts (8-ply).

Purl 1 row.
Change to red and work 2 rows st st.
Change to blue and work 2 rows st st.
Change to green and work 2 rows st st.
Change to yellow and work **picot edge picot ro**w:
k1, *yfwd, k2tog, rep from * to last 2 sts, k2.
Work another row yellow.
Change to green and work 2 rows st st.
Change to blue and work 2 rows st st.
Change to red and work 2 rows st st.
Change to red and work 2 rows st st.
Next row: Wth right side facing and using
orange, fold up hem at picot edge row and knit
1 st from needle together with 1 loop from
cast-on edge until all sts have been worked.

Commence Pattern using orange.
Row 1: Knit.
Row 2 and 4: Purl.
Row 3: P1, *k, p, k all into same st, p3tog, rep
from * to last st, p1.
Row 5: P1, *p3tog, k, p, k all into same st, rep
from * to last st, p1.
Row 6: Purl.
These 6rows orm pattern.
Continue in pattern until work measures 17 cm
from picot row ending with a row 6.

Commence Decrease
Next row: P1, *p1, p3tog, rep from * to end.
Next row: K2tog all across.
Break off yarn thread through rem sts. Pull up

tightly and fasten off.
Make 2.
To Make Up With right sides together, stitch the
top seam together working from the top centre
point down, 5–6 cm each side. Turn right side out.

Handle and Spout Openings
Using 4 mm knitting needles and orange, and
with the right side facing, pick up and knit 48 (55)
sts along both edges of each piece. Work 1 more
row in orange. Work 8 rows in red and 2 more in
orange. Cast off.

To Make Up Cosy Fold piece to the wrong side
and stitch in place. Stitch together the bottom
seam for 3–4 cm.
Darn in any loose ends.

CATERPILLAR
Using 2.75 mm knitting needles and bright green,
cast on 12 sts.
Row 1: Knit
Row 2: P10, wrap.
Row 3: K8 , wrap.
Row 4: P6, wrap.
Row 5: K4, wrap.
Row 6: Purl.
Repeat these 6 rows another 4 times. Cast off.
With right sides together, sew side seam half
way. Turn right side out and stuff firmly. Sew the
rest of the seam and then run a gathering thread
around the cast-on edge. Pull up firmly and
fasten off. Do the same with the other end. Make
sure you have sufficient filling and have a round,
firm ball. Make 4 in bright green and 3 in olive
green.

For the head, use red and cast on 14 sts. Work in the same manner as for the green balls:

Row 1: Knit

Row 2: P12, wrap.

Row 3: K10 , wrap.

Row 4: P8, wrap.

Row 5: K6, wrap.

Row 6: Purl.

Complete as for the bright green balls.

To Make Up Sew the balls together, alternating the bright and olive green balls and finishing with the red head.

Embroider the eyes using yellow embroidery thread. Make a green bullion knot in the centre.

Antennae

Using 2.75 mm knitting needles and brown DK (8-ply), cast on 5 sts. Cast off. Make 2. Stitch firmly to the top of the head.

LEAVES

Using 2.75 mm double-pointed knitting needles and bright green cast 3 sts. Work an I-cord for 1.5 cm.

Row 1: Knit.

Row 2: Knit.

Row 3: K1, m1, k1, m1, k1.

Row 4 and all even rows: Knit.

Row 5: K2, m1, k1, m1, k2.

Row 7: K3 m1, k1, m1, k3.

Row 9: K4, m1, k1, m1, k4.

Row 11: K5, m1, k1, m1, k5.

Rows 13–17: Knit

Row 18: K5, sl2, k1, psso, k5.

Row 19: K4, sl2, k1, psso, k4.

Row 21: K3, sl2, k1, psso, k3.

Row 23: K2, sl2, k1, psso, k2.

Rows 24 and 26: Purl.

Row 25: K1, sl2, k1, psso, k1 (3 sts).

Row 27: K1, sl2, psso, fasten off.

Make 2 in bright green and 2 in olive green.

To Decorate The Cosy Sew 2 leaves to each side of the tea cosy. Sew the caterpillar firmly on the top.

Warm and Toastie Mouse

Sitting on top of this sumptuous striped tea cosy is a sweet little mouse wearing a nightcap, who's all ready for bed. Surrounded by hot water bottles, he has an extravagant requirement for warmth, as well as a desire to live in luxury. The basic cosy body is a traditional shape made by pulling up the wool colour not being used when the stripes are knitted.

SIZE
To fit a 6-cup teapot

MATERIALS
2 x 50 g balls blue DK (8 ply)
2 x 50 g balls cream DK (8 ply)
Small amount of 4-ply wool or
    cotton in shades of blue
Small amount of fawn 4-ply
    cotton
Small amount of pink 4-ply
Stranded embroidery cotton
    in pink and black
Polyester fibre filling
1 pair 4 mm knitting needles
4 x 2.25 mm double-pointed
    knitting needles
1 pair 2 mm knitting needles
Wool needle

Note The pleated fabric is created by pulling the yarn not in use tightly across on the wrong side. It is important to do this on each row. Carry the yarn on the back of the work and right to the ends. It may seem a little slow to begin with but you will develop a rhythm.

Using 4 mm knitting needles and blue (A) DK (8-ply) wool, cast on 98 sts. Work 8 rows garter st (every row knit). Join in cream (B).
Row 1: K1A, k6B, *k7A, k7B, rep from * to last 7 sts, k6A, k1B. As you knit, pull the yarn not in use very firmly behind to draw up the pleats.
Row 2: K1B, k6A, *k7B, k6A, rep from * to last 7 sts, k6B, k1A. Keep yarn to the front in this row and pull the yarn not in use tightly so that the pleats remain firm.
These 2 rows form pattern. Continue in pattern until 48 rows have been worked.

Commence Decreases
Row 1: (rs) K2togA, k3B, k2togB, *k2togA, k3B, k2togB, k3B, k2togB, rep from * to last 7 sts, k2togA, k3A, k2togB.
Row 2: K1B, K4A, *k5B, k5A, rep from * to last 5 sts, k4B, k1A.
Row 3: K2togA, k1B, k2togB, *k2togA, k1A, k2togA, k2togB, k1B, k2togB rep from * to last 5 sts, k2togA, k1A, k2togB.
Row 4: K1B, k2A, *k3B, k3A, rep from * to last 3 sts, k2B, k1A.
Row 5: K2togA, k1B, *k2togA, k1A, k2togB, k1B, rep from * to last 3 sts, k2togA, k1B.
Row 6: K1B, k1A, *k2B, k2A, rep from *to last 2 sts, k1B, k1A.
Row 7: (K2togA) twice, *k2togB, k2togA, rep from

* to last 4 sts, (k2togB) twice.
Break off yarn, thread through rem sts, pull up tightly and fasten off.
Make 2.

To Make Up Darn in any loose ends. With right sides together, stitch from the centre top down each side for 5 cm. Tie off very firmly. Join sides together at the bottom edge, stitching up each side for 3–4 cm. Turn right side out.

HOT WATER BOTTLE
Using 2 mm knitting needles and blue 4-ply, cast on 8 sts. Work 2 rows garter st.
Row 3: Inc at each end (10 sts).
Row 4: K1, purl to last st, k1.
Row 5: Inc at each end (12 sts).
Row 6: K1, purl to last st, k1.
Work another 12 rows garter st without shaping, keeping garter st border correct on purl rows.
Row 19: Sl1, k1, psso, knit to last 2 sts, k2tog.
Row 20: K1, purl to last st, K1.
Row 21: Sl1, k1, psso, knit to last 2 sts, k2tog.
Row 22: K1, purl to last st, k1.
Work 2 rows garter st. Cast off.
Make 2 for each hot water bottle. Make 8–10 hot water bottles in different shades of blue.

Stopper
Using 2 mm knitting needles and blue 4-ply, cast on 18 sts. Work 2 rows st st beginning with a purl row.
Row 3: P2tog all across. Break off yarn, thread through rem sts, pull up tightly and fasten off. Join row ends together to form a neat round.

To Make Up Place right sides of bottle together and stitch closed leaving top open. Turn right side out. Push a small amount of polyester fibre filling inside. Position stopper in the middle of the top of the hot water bottle and stitch firmly closed. Stitch across the top of the bottle.

MOUSE
Head
Use 2.25 mm double-pointed knitting needles and fawn cotton, cast on 9 sts, (3, 3, 3). Join into a ring without twisting stitches.

Round 1: Knit.
Round 2: K1, m1, k1, on each needle (15 sts).
Round 3: Knit.
Round 4: K1, m1, k3, m1, k1 (21 sts).
Rounds 5–8: Knit.
Round 9: K1, k2tog, k1, k2tog, k1 (15 sts).
Rounds 10–11: Knit.
Round 12: Sl1, k1, psso, k1, k2tog (9 sts).
Round 13: Knit.

Leaving sts on needle, stuff head firmly. Run thread through rem sts, pull up tightly and fasten off. Set aside.

Body
Using 2.25 mm double-pointed knitting needles and white cotton, cast on 9 sts (3, 3, 3). Join into a ring.

Round 1: Knit.
Round 2: K1, m1, k1, on each needle (15 sts)
Round 3: Knit.
Round 4: K1, m1, k3, m1, k1 (21 sts).
Round 5: Knit.
Round 6: K1, m1, k5, m1, k1 (27 sts).
Rounds 7–15: Knit.

Round 16: Sl1, k1, psso, k5, k2tog on each needle (21 sts).
Round 17: Knit.
Round 18: Sl1, k1, psso, k3, k2tog, on each needle (15 sts).
Round 19: Knit.
Round 20: Sl1, k1, psso, k1, k2tog, on each needle (9 sts).
Round 21: Knit.

Leaving sts on needle, stuff body firmly. Run thread through rem sts, pull up tightly and fasten off. Set aside for later.

Ears
Use 2.25 mm double-pointed knitting needles and work backwards and forwards in rows.
Cast on 2 sts **Row 1 and 3**: Purl.
Row 2: K1, m1, k1.
Row 4: Purl, inc in first and last st.
Work 2 rows without shaping.
Row 7: K2tog, k1, k2tog.
Row 8: Purl.
Cast off.

To Make Up Using 3 strands of pink embroidery cotton and satin stitch, embroider the inner surface of the ear. To attach to head, pinch lower edges together and pin in place. When you are happy with the arrangement sew firmly to the head.

I-Cord Arms and Legs
The legs and arms are made with knitted I-cords. Using 2.25 mm double-pointed knitting needles and fawn 4-ply cotton, cast on 3 sts.
Row 1: Knit.

Do not turn, slide sts to the other end of the needle, pull yarn firmly behind the work and repeat the row. Continue in this manner until the I-cord is 3 cm long for each of the arms and 4 cm long for each of the legs.

Next row: Sl1, k2tog, psso, fasten off.

Paws

These are bobbles that are stitched to the end of the leg or the arm.

Using 2.25 mm double-pointed knitting needles and fawn 4-ply cotton, cast on 1 st.

Row 1: K, p, k, p, k, into this stitch, making 5 stitches.

Row 2: Turn. Purl

Row 3: Turn. Knit.

Row 4: Turn. Purl.

Row 5: Turn. Knit, Do not turn, Slip the second stitch over the first stitch on the right-hand needle. Continue in this manner until 1 st rem. Break off yarn. Thread through st. Pull up tightly and fasten off. Run a gathering stitch around the outside, draw up and fasten off, forming into a bobble. Make 4. Attach one to each arm and leg.

To Make Up Sew the head to the body with the pointy nose facing forwards and the widest part of the body as the base. Using 3 strands of black embroidery cotton, make a French knot on each side of the head for the eyes and fasten off where the head joins the body. Using the pink embroidery cotton, make a French knot on the nose. Sew arms at shoulder height and legs at hip height. Make sure you attach all parts firmly.

Tail

Make a 2-stitch I-cord 6 cm long. Sew in place.

Hat

Using 2 mm knitting needles and blue 4-ply, cast on 12 sts. Work in stripes of 2 rows blue and 2 rows white.

With blue work 2 rows st st.

With white work 1 row purl for hem, then 1 more row purl.

Work 2 rows blue, then 2 rows white.

Commence Decrease

Sl1, k1, psso, knit to last 2 sts, k2tog,

P1 row.

Rep this sequence of decreases, keeping stripe pattern correct, until 3 sts rem. Cast off.

To Make Up Fold hat in half and carefully sew seam. Fold hem to the inside and place nightcap on head. Stitch in place. Darn in any ends.

TO FINISH

Place cosy on the teapot. Position seated mouse on the top of the cosy. Surround him with all his hot water bottles. Pin in place, then when you are happy with the arrangement, stitch to secure each.

Under Green Willow

Knitted leaves in different shades of green and yellow create an impressive jungle camouflage to keep your teapot away from the prying eyes of non-tea lovers. The leaves also give the perfect opportunity to use up those oddments of leaf-coloured yarn. The leaves are not difficult to knit and once you've mastered the technique, it provides a meditative activity.

SIZE
To fit a 6-cup teapot

MATERIALS
2 x 50 g balls of bright green DK (8-ply) wool
5 or 6 part balls in shades of green DK (8-ply) wool
2 x 2.75 mm double-pointed knitting needles
5 x 4 mm double-pointed knitting needles
Wool needle

Using 3 x 4 mm double-pointed knitting needles and bright green, cast on 90 sts (30, 30, 30). Join into a ring, being careful not to twist the stitches. Work 5 rounds st st (every round knit).

Picot round: *Yfwd, k2tog, rep from * to end of round.

Work another 5 rounds st st.

Round 12 Fold hem at picot round and knit 1 stitch from needle together with 1 loop from cast-on edge until all stitches have been worked. Work another 5 cm in st st from picot round.

Divide for Spout and Handle Openings

Next round: Place stitch marker. Knit first 45 sts on to 1needle. These will become the first side. Knit the remaining 45 sts onto another needle. You will now be knitting backwards and forwards in rows on the first 45 sts. Turn.

Next row: K4, purl to last 4 sts, k4.

Next row: Knit.

Rep the last 2 rows until work measures 16 cm from beg. Break off yarn.

Rejoin yarn and work other side to match, keeping garter stitch border correct.

Once both sides are complete, redistribute the stitches evenly back on to three needles ready to commence top shaping. Ensure that round starts with the stitch marker.

Shape Top

Round 1: *K7, k2tog, rep from * to end.

Round 2 and all even rounds: Knit.

Round 3: *K6, k2tog, rep from * to end.

Round 5: *K5, k2tog, rep from * to end.

Keeping pattern of decreases, continue in this manner until the round k1, k2tog has been worked. Break off yarn. Thread through rem sts, pull up tight and fasten off.

To Make Up Darn in all loose ends.

LEAVES

Using 2.75 mm double-pointed knitting needles and a green oddment, cast on 3 sts. Work an I-cord for 1.5 cm.

Row 1: Knit.

Row 2: Purl.

Row 3: K1, m1, k1, m1, k1.

Row 4 and all even rows: K1, purl to last st, k1.

Row 5: K2, m1, k1, m1, k2.

Row 7: K3 m1, k1, m1, k3.

Row 9: K4, m1, k1, m1, k4.

Row 11: K5, m1, k1, m1, k5.

Rows 13 and 15: Knit.

Row 17: K5, sl2, k1, psso, k5.

Row 19: K4, sl2, k1, psso, k4.

Row 21: K3, sl2, k1, psso, k3.

Row 23: K2, sl2, k1, psso, k2.

Rows 24 and 26: Purl.

Row 25: K1, sl2, k1, psso, k1 (3 sts).

Row 27: K1, sl2, psso, fasten off.

Make at least 45.

To Make Up Put the cosy onto the teapot. Pin the leaves in place in a random colour arrangement. Start sewing the leaves from the base upwards. Save one leaf to put on top to cover any stems. More is always better.

Woodland Gnome Comes to Tea

This little gnome is right at home among the autumn leaves that adorn the sides of this cute tea cosy. He is not difficult to make – the body and head are knitted in one piece and the arms and legs are made of I-cords and added after the body is stuffed. The beard can be made with any leftover mohair or other fancy yarn. Take your time stuffing the body so you achieve a plump shape.

SIZE
To fit a 6-cup teapot

MATERIALS
2 x 50 g balls beige chunky
  (12-ply) or DK (8-ply) wool
1 x 50 g ball mid-brown chunky
  (12-ply) or DK (8-ply) woo
1 pair 4 mm knitting needles
Wool needle
Small amounts of 4-ply wool in
  crimson and pink
1 x 25 g ball variegated
  pink 4-ply wool
Tiny amount of mohair or
  eyelash yarn
1 pair 2 mm knitting needles
2 x 2.25 mm double-pointed
  knitting needles
Polyester fibre filling
Small amounts of fawn, brown,
  cream and 3 or 4 shades of
  green DK (8-ply) yarn
2 x 2.75 mm double-pointed
  knitting needles

Note DK (8 ply) pattern is given in brackets.

Using 4 mm knitting needles, cast on 46 sts (12-ply) or 54 sts (8-ply).
Beginning with a knit row and dark brown, work 6 (8) rows st st.
Picot row: K1, *Yfwd, k2tog, rep from * to last 2 sts, k2.
Beginning with a purl row, work another 7 (9) rows st st.
Next row: Wth right side facing, fold up hem at picot row and knit 1 st from needle together with loop from cast-on edge until all sts have been worked off. Break off brown and join in beige.
Row 1: Knit.
Rows 2, 4 and 6: Purl.
Row 3: P1, *k, p, k all into same st, p3tog, rep from * to last st, p1.
Row 5: P1, *p3tog, k, p, k all into same st, rep from * to last st, p1.
These 6 rows form pattern.
Continue in pattern until work measures 17 cm from picot row ending with a row 6 pattern.
Commence decrease for top.
Next row: P1, *p1, p3tog, rep from * to end.
Next row: K2tog all across.
Break off yarn thread through rem sts. Pull up tightly and fasten off.

To Make Up With right sides together, carefully stitch the top seam closed, working from the centre point 5–6 cm down each side. Turn right side out.

Handle and Spout Openings
Using 4 mm knitting needles and 12-ply (8-ply) wool, and with the right side facing, pick up and knit 48 (55) sts along both pieces. Work 12 rows st st. Cast off.

To Make Up Fold the piece in half to the wrong side and stitch in place. Stitch the bottom seam for 3–4 cm. Sew in any loose ends.

GNOME
Using three 2.25 mm double-pointed knitting needles and pink 4-ply for head, cast on 9 sts (3, 3, 3). Join into a ring, being careful not to twist sts.
Knit one round.
Round 2: Inc in every st (18 sts).
Work 2 rounds st st.
Round 5: Inc in every st (36 sts).
Work 2 rounds st st.
Round 8: *K1, inc in next st, rep from * to end (54 sts).
Work 2 rounds st st.
Round 11: *Sl1, k1, psso, rep from * to end.
Knit 2 rounds.
Round 14: *Sl1, k1, psso, rep from * to end (18 sts).
Work 4 rounds st st.
Break off pink and join in variegated pink.
Work 2 rounds st st.
Round 21: *K1, inc in next st, rep from* to end (27 sts).
Work 2 rounds st st.
Round 24: *K1, inc in next st, rep from* to end (40 sts).
Work another 10 rounds st st.
Round 35: *K5, m1, rep from * to end (50 sts).
Work 3 rounds st st.

Round 39: *K2, k2tog, k1, rep from * to end.
Work 3 rounds st st.
Round 43: *K1, k2tog, k2, rep from * to end.
Work 2 rounds st st.
Round 46: K2tog all round.

To Make Up With sts still on needles, stuff head and body firmly with polyester fibre filling, ensuring that the body is a plump shape. Break off yarn, thread through rem sts, pull up tightly and fasten off. With pink yarn, run a gathering thread around the neck to give the head more definition. Tie off the ends invisibly in the body.

Hat

Using 2 mm knitting needles and crimson 4-ply, cast on 32 sts. Beginning with a knit row, work 4 rows st st.
Row 5: Purl.
Beginning with a purl row work 6 rows st st.
Row 12: *K2, k2tog, k2, rep from * ending with k2.
Work 3 rows st st.
Row 16: *K2, k2tog, k1, rep from * ending with k2tog.
Work 5 rows st st.
Row 22: *K1, k2tog, rep from * to end.
Work 5 rows st st.
Row 28: K2tog 5 times, k1.
Work 5 rows st st.
Row 34: K2tog 3 times.
Switch to double-pointed knitting needles and continue working rem 3 sts into an I-cord until point of hat measures 8 cm.
Sl1, k2tog, psso. Fasten off.
To Make Up Carefully sew centre back seam

closed, then fold brim to the outside, catching it in position using very small stitches.

Beard

Using 2 mm knitting needles and mohair or eyelash yarn, cast on 1 st.
Row 1: Inc in st.
Row 2: K1, inc in next st (3 sts).
Inc at beg and end of each of the following rows until there are 15 sts.
Knit 1 row.
Cast off.

To Make Up Sew in position across lower part of face. It should fit neatly more than half way around the head.

Nose

Using 2.25 mm double-pointed knitting needles and pink 4-ply yarn, cast on 1 st.
K, p, k, p into same st (4 sts).
Turn. Purl.
Turn. Knit.
Turn. Purl.
Turn. Knit.
Do not turn. Slip second st over the first st, and repeat this process until 1 st remains. Fasten off.

To Make Up Run a gathering thread around the bobble and form into a neat circle. Attach centrally to the face just above the beard.

Legs and Boots

Using 2.25 mm double-pointed knitting needles and crimson 4-ply yarn, cast on 2 sts.
Row 1: Purl.

Row 2: Inc in each st.
Row 3 and every odd row: Purl.
Row 4: P1, inc in next 2 sts, p1.
Row 6: P2, inc in next 2 sts, p2.
Cont inc in centre 2 sts in this manner until there are 12 sts.
Next row: Purl 1 row.
Next row: K6, sl1, k1, psso, turn, p2, p2tog, turn, k2, sl1, k1, psso, turn, p2, p2tog, turn, k2, sl1, k1, psso, turn, p2, p2tog, Continue in this manner until 4 sts rem.
Break off crimson and join in variegated pink 4-ply yarn for leg. Work a 4-st I-cord for 6 cm. K2 tog twice.
Next row: K2tog. Fasten off.
Make 2.

Arms

Using 2.25 mm double-pointed knitting needles and variegated 4-ply yarn, cast on 4 sts. Work a 4-st I-ord for 5.5 cm. K2tog twice.
Next row: K2tog. Fasten off.
Make 2.

To Make Up Stitch legs to each side of the body ensuring that the toes of the boots are pointing forwards. Stitch the arms to each side of the top of the body just below the neck.

LEAVES

Using 2.75 mm double-pointed knitting needles and green DK (8-ply), cast 3 sts. Work an I-cord for 1.5 cm.
Row 1: Knit.
Row 2: Purl.
Row 3: K1, m1, K1, m1, k1.

Row 4 and all even rows: K first and last st and purl rem sts.
Row 5: K2, m1, k1, m1, k2.
Row 7: K3 m1, k1, m1, k3.
Row 19: K4, m1, k1, m1, k4.
Row 11: K5, m1, k1, m1, k5.
Rows 13 and 15: Knit.
Row 17: K5, sl2, k1, psso, k5.
Row 19: K4, sl2, k1, psso, k4.
Row 21: K3, sl2, k1, psso, k3.
Row 23: K2, sl2, k1, psso, k2.
Rows 24 and 26: Purl.
Row 25: K1, sl2, k1, psso, k1.
Row 27: K1, sl2, psso. Fasten off.
Make 4.

MUSHROOM
Cap

Using 2.25 mm knitting needles and fawn 4-ply, cast on 3 sts,
Row 1: (K1, yo) twice, k1 (5 sts).
Row 2: (P1, p1tbl) twice, p1.
Row 3: (K1, yo) 4 times, k1 (9 sts).
Rows 4, 6 and 8: (P1, p1tbl) to last st, p1.
Row 5: (K1, yo) 8 times, k1 (17 sts).
Row 7: (K1, yo) 16 times, k1 (33 sts).
Row 9: (K3, yo) 10 times, k3 (43 sts).
Row 10: Purl, working each yo as p1tbl.
Row 11: Knit.
Row 12: Purl** change to dark brown yarn.
Rows 13 and 14: Knit.
***Row 15**: Knit.
Row 16: (P1, k2) to last st, k1.
Row 17: (P1, p2tog), to last st, k1 (29 sts).
Row 18: (P1, k1), to last st, p1.
Row 19: (K1, sl1, psso) 7 times, k1 (15 sts).

Row 20: As row 18.
Row 21: (K1, sl1, psso) 7 times, k1 (8 sts)****
Stalk
Beginning with a purl row, work 9 rows st st.
Row 31: (K2, yo) 3 times, k2 (11 sts).
Row 32: As row 10.
Row 33: Knit.
Row 34: Purl.
Row 35: K1, (k2tog) 5 times. Cast off.

To Make Up Gather base. Taking in half a stitch
from each edge join side seam with ladder stitch.
Fill firmly with polyester fibre filling.

Truly Madly Tea Party

Here is another fantasy cosy inspired by *Alice in Wonderland's* famous tea party with the Hatter and his eccentric companions. Here we have the White Rabbit taking centre stage, surrounded by oversized and overfilled teacups. The refreshing palette of blue and white yarn gives the stripy design a zany seaside feel. Experienced knitters will be able to scale up, or scale down, the emellishments.

SIZE
To fit a 6-cup teapot

MATERIALS
2 x 50 g balls blue DK
    (8-ply) wool
2 x 50 g balls cream DK
    (8-ply) wool
1 pair 4 mm knitting needles
1 x 50 g ball of white
    4-ply cotton
1 x 50 g ball of blue 4-ply cotton
Small amount of beige
    4-ply cotton
4 x 2.25 mm double-pointed
    knitting needles
1 pair 2 mm knitting needles
Stranded embroidery thread in
    pink and black
Wool needle
Polyester fibre filling

Note The pleated fabric is created by pulling the yarn not in use tightly across on the wrong side. It is important to do this on each row. Carry the yarn on the back of the work and right across to the ends. It may seem a little slow to begin with but you will develop a rhythm.

Using 4 mm knitting needles and blue (A) DK (8-ply) wool, cast on 98 sts. Work 8 rows garter st (every row knit). Join in cream (B) DK (8-ply) wool.

Row 1: K1A, k6B, *k7A, k7B, rep from * to last 7 sts, k6A, k1B. As you knit, pull the yarn not in use very firmly behind to draw up the pleats.

Row 2: K1B, k6A, *k7B, k6A, rep from * to last 7 sts, k6B, k1A. Keep yarn to the front in this row and continue to pull the yarn not in use tightly so that pleats remain firm.

These 2 rows form pattern. Continue in pattern until 48 rows have been worked.

Commence Decreases

Row 3: (rs) K2togA, k3B, k2togB, *k2togA, k3A, k2togB, k3B, k2togB, rep from * to last 7 sts, k2togA, k3A, k2togB.

Row 2: K1B, k4A, *k5B, k5A, rep from * to last 5 sts, k4B, k1A.

Row 3: K2togA, k1B, k2togB, *k2togA, k1A, k2togA, k2togB, k1B, k2togB rep from * to last 5 sts, k2togA, k1A, k2togB.

Row 4: K1B, k2A, *k3B, k3A, rep from * to last 3 sts, k2B, k1A.

Row 5: K2togA, k1B, *k2togA, k1A, k2togB, k1B, rep from * to last 3 sts, k2togA, k1B.

Row 6: K1B, k1A, *k2B, k2A, rep from *to last 2 sts, k1B, k1A.

Row 7: (K2togA) twice, *k2togB, k2togA, rep from * to last 4 sts, (k2togB) twice.
Break off yarn, thread through rem sts, pull up tightly and fasten off.
Make 2.

To Make Up Darn in any loose ends. With right sides together, stitch the two halves together working from the centre top down each side for 5 cm. Tie off firmly. Join sides together at the bottom edge, stitching up each side for 3–4 cm. Turn right side out.

TEA CUPS
Cup
Using 2 mm knitting needles and blue 4-ply cotton, cast on 39 sts.
Work 2 rows st st.
Picot row: *K1, sl1, k1, psso, rep from * to last st, k1.
Beginning with a purl row, work another 5 rows st st.
Row 4: K4, *K2tog, k3, rep from * to end.
Row 5: Purl.
Row 6: K4, *k2tog, k2, rep from * to end.
Row 7: Purl.
Row 8: K3, *k2tog, k1, rep from * to end.
Row 9–11: Purl.
Row 12: K2tog all across.
Break off yarn, thread through rem sts, pull up tightly and fasten off.
Make 3.
Fold the hem above the picot row of the cup to the inside and stitch in place. Sew the short ends together to make a tube.

Saucer

Using 2 mm knitting needles and blue 4-ply cotton, cast on 55 sts. Work 2 rows st st beginning with a knit row.

Picot row: *K1, sl1, k1, psso, rep from * to end.
Work another 3 rows st st beginning with a purl row.

Row 4: *K2, k2tog, k1, rep from * to end.
Row 5: Purl.
Row 6: Knit.
Row 7: * P1, p2tog, p1, rep from * to end.
Row 8: Knit.
Row 9: Purl.
Row 10: *K1, k2tog, rep from * to end.
Row 11: Purl.
Row 12: K2tog all across.
Break off yarn, thread through rem sts, pull up tightly and fasten off.
Stitch the short raw edges together. Fold the picot row of the saucer to the outside edge and stitch in place.

Handle

Using 2 x 2.25 mm double-pointed knitting needles and blue 4-ply cotton, cast on 3 sts.
Make an I-cord 2 cm long. Fasten off.

Tea

Using 2 mm knitting needles and beige 4-ply cotton, cast on 45 sts.
Beginning with a purl row, st st 4 rows.
Row 5 and 6: Knit.
Row 7 and all odd rows: Purl.
Row 8: *K3, k2tog, rep from * to end.
Row 10: *K2, k2tog, rep from * to end.
Row 12: * K1, k2tog, rep from * to end.

Row 14: K2tog all across.
Break off yarn, thread through rem sts, pull up tightly and fasten off.

To Make Up Press lightly to flatten and then oversew the row ends together. Turn the edge inwards so that it lies flat.
Fill the cup with a little polyester fibre filling and put the tea on top, matching the edges. Stitch all around the outer edge, enclosing the filling with tiny, invisible stitches. Sew the bottom of the cup to the saucer.

RABBIT

Use white 4-ply cotton and 2.25 mm double-pointed knitting needles.

Head

Cast on 9 sts (3, 3, 3). Join into a ring.
Round 1: Knit.
Round 2: K1, m1, k1, on each needle (15 sts)
Round 3: Knit.
Round 4: K1, m1, k3, m1, k1 (21 sts).
Rounds 5–8: Knit.
Round 9: K1, k2tog, k1, k2tog, k1 (15 sts).
Rounds 10 and 11: Knit.
Round 12: Sl1, k1, psso, k1, k2tog (9 sts).
Round 13: Knit.
Leaving sts on needle, stuff head firmly. Run thread through rem sts, pull up tightly and fasten off. Set aside.

Body

Cast on 9 sts (3, 3, 3). Join into a ring.
Round 1: Knit.
Round 2: K1, m1, k1, on each needle (15 sts).

Round 3: Knit.
Round 4: K1, m1, k3, m1, k1 (21 sts).
Round 5: Knit.
Round 6: K1, m1, k5, m1, k1 (27 sts).
Rounds 7–15: Knit.
Round 16: Sl1, k1, psso, k5, k2tog on each needle (21 sts).
Round 17: Knit.
Round 18: Sl1, k1, psso, k3, k2tog, on each needle (15 sts).
Round 19: Knit.
Round 20: Sl1, k1, psso, k1, k2tog, on each needle (9 sts).
Round 21: Knit.
Leaving sts on needle, stuff body firmly. Run thread through rem sts, pull up tightly and fasten off. Set aside.

Ears
Using 2.25 mm double-pointed knitting needles and working backwards and forwards in rows, cast on 2 sts.
Row 1 and all odd rows: Purl.
Row 2: K1, m1, k1.
Row 4: K1, m1, k1, m1, k1.
Work 15 rows st st ending with a purl row.
Next row: K2tog, k1, k2tog.
Next row: Purl.
Cast off. Make 2.

I-Cord Legs and Arms
Make 2 arms, each 3 cm long, and 2 legs, each 4 cm long.
Using 2.25 mm double-pointed knitting needles and white 4-ply cotton, cast on 3 sts.
Knit 1 row. Do not turn, slide sts to the other end of the needle, pull yarn firmly behind the work and repeat the first row. Continue in this manner until your I-cord is the desired length.
To finish, sl1, k2tog, psso, fasten off.

Feet, Paws and Tail
Cast on 1 st.
Knit, purl, knit, purl, knit, into this stitch (5 sts). Turn. Purl. Turn. Knit. Turn. Purl. Turn. Knit. Do not turn. Slip the second stitch over the first stitch on the right-hand needle. Continue in this manner until 1 st remains. Break off yarn. Thread through st. Pull up tightly and fasten off. To form into a bobble, run a gathering stitch around the outside, draw up and fasten off, forming into a circle. Attach one to each arm and leg and keep one for the tail.

To Make Up Sew head to body with pointy nose facing forwards. Pin ears to each side of head and sew in place.
Using 3 strands of pink embroidery cotton work a few short stitches across and one or two down for the nose.
To embroider the eyes, use 3 strands of black stranded cotton and work a couple of short stitches or make a French knot. Tie off where the body attaches to the head so the knot will be hidden.

SCARF
Using 2 mm knitting needles and blue 4-ply cotton, cast on 45 sts.
Knit 1 row. Cast off.
Sew in ends. Knot around rabbit's neck.

To Decorate the Cosy Position the three tea cups at random around the tea cosy, with one near to the top. Centre the sitting rabbit on top of the tea cosy. Stitch firmly in place using small stitches and matching thread.

Heavenly Roses

This tea cosy uses a blackberry stitch and a blackberry-coloured yarn. The pale pink and lilac roses offer a sublime finish to this elegant floral creation. You can easily introduce quite a different mood by using your own colours and textures.

SIZE
To fit a 6-cup teapot

MATERIALS
2 x 50 g balls of dark purple DK (8-ply) or chunky (12-ply) wool
1 x 50 g ball of variegated purple DK (8-ply) wool
1 x 50 g ball of mauve DK (8-ply) wool
1 x 50 g ball of bright purple DK (8-ply) wool
1 pair 4 mm knitting needles
3 mm crochet hook
Wool needle

Note DK 8-ply version is given in brackets.

Using 4 mm knitting needles and dark purple, cast on 46 sts (12 ply) or 54 sts (8 ply). Commencing with a knit row work 6 (8) rows st st.

Picot edge row: K1, *yfwd, k2tog, rep from * to last 2 sts, k2.

Commencing with a purl row work another 7 (9) rows st st.

Next row: Wth right side facing, fold up hem at picot edge row and knit 1 st together with loop from cast-on edge until all sts have been worked.

Commence Pattern

Row 1: Knit.

Row 2 and all even rows: Purl.

Row 3: P1, *k, p, k all into same st, p3tog, rep from * to last st, p1.

Row 5: P1, *p3tog, k, p, k all into same st, rep from * to last st, p1.

Row 6: Purl.

These 5 rows form pattern.

Continue in pattern until work measures 17 cm from picot edge ending with a row 6.

Commence Decrease

Next row: P1, *p1, p3tog, rep from * to end.

Next row: K2tog all across.

Break off yarn, thread through rem sts. Pull up tightly and fasten off.

To Make Up With right sides together, carefully stitch the top seam closed, from the centre point and 5-6 cm down each side. Turn right side out.

Handle and Spout Openings

Using 4 mm knitting needles and 12-ply (8-ply) wool and with right side facing, pick up and knit 48 (55) sts along both pieces.
Work 12 rows st st. Cast off.

To Make Up Fold piece to the wrong side and carefully stitch in place. Stitch from the bottom seam for 3–4 cm. Sew in any loose ends.

ROSES

Using 3 mm crochet hook and purple DK (8-ply), make 48ch. Turn, and miss 4 ch, dtr into next 43ch, tr into last ch.

Next row: 3ch, 3tr into each dtr, to last 2 sts, 1 dbl, sl into last tr.

Fasten off.

Starting at the end with the sl st and dbl crochet, roll the rose up, securing with small stitches at the base.

Make at least 6 in different shades of purple. Attach one to the top centre of the tea cosy and arrange the others radiating out. The more flowers you have the more luscious the tea cosy will look.

Winter Roses

This sumpptuous, one-colour tea cosy creates an effusive symphony of cream with its beautiful roses, and would make a perfect wedding gift. It would also be a lovely cosy for an afternoon tea, served with tiny sandwiches, scones with jam and cream and elegant white china. It is knitted in chunky (12-ply) yarn, and the roses are crocheted in DK (8-ply) mohair.

SIZE
To fit a 6-cup teapot

MATERIALS
2 x 50 g balls of cream chunky (12-ply) wool
1 x 50 g ball of cream DK (8-ply) mohair
Small amount cream DK (8-ply) wool
5 x 4 mm double-pointed knitting keedles
3 mm crochet hook
1 pair 3 mm knitting needles
Wool needle

Using three 4 mm double-pointed knitting needles and chunky (12-ply) yarn, cast on 90 sts (30, 30, 30). Join into a ring, being careful not to twist the stitches.

Work 5 rounds st st (every round knit).

Picot round: *Yfwd, k2tog, rep from * to end of round.

Work another 5 rounds st st.

Round 12 Fold hem at picot round and knit 1 stitch from needle together with 1 loop from cast-on edge until all stitches have been worked. Work another 5 cm in st st.

Divide for Spout and Handle Openings

Next round: Place stitch marker. Knit first 45 sts on to 1 needle. These will become the first side. Knit the remaining 45 sts onto another needle. You will now be knitting backwards and forwards in rows on the first 45 sts. Turn.

Next row: K4, purl to last 4 sts, k4.

Next row: Knit.

Rep the last 2 rows until work measures 16 cm from beg. Break off yarn.

Rejoin yarn and work other side to match, keeping garter stitch border correct.

Once both sides are complete, redistribute stitches evenly back on to three needles ready to commence top shaping. Ensure that round starts with stitch marker.

Shape Top

Round 1: *K7, k2 tog, rep from * to end.

Round 2 and all even rounds: Knit.

Round 3: *K6, k2tog, rep from * to end.

Round 5: *K5, k2tog, rep from * to end.

Keeping pattern of decreases, continue in this manner until the round k1, k2tog has been worked. Break off yarn. Thread through rem sts, pull up tight and fasten off.

To Make Up the Cosy Sew in all loose ends.

ROSES

Using 3 mm crochet hook and cream DK (8-ply) mohair, make 48ch. Turn, and miss 4 ch, dtr into next 43ch, tr into last ch.

Next row: 3ch, 3tr into each dtr, to last 2 sts, 1 dbl, sl into last tr.

Fasten off.

Starting at the end with the sl st and dbl crochet, roll the rose up, securing with small stitches at the base.

Make at least 9. The more flowers you have the more luscious your tea cosy will look.

TWISTED CORDS

Using 3.75mm knitting needles and cream dk, cast on 25 sts.

Inc into every st (50 sts).

Knit 1 row. Cast off purlwise.

To Decorate the Cosy Attach one rose to the centre top of the tea cosy and the remainder radiating outwards. Stitch on the twisted cords.

Timeless Tea Cosy

This is an old-fashioned tea cosy and follows the basic shape of many of the decorated tea cosies in this book. With its thick pleated fabric it is very insulating, keeping your tea hot. The pleated structure also provides a firm, stable surface on which to attach knitted embellishments. Be sure to use pure wool, not acrylic as it is far more insulating and acrylic is harder on the hands.

SIZE
To fit a 6-cup teapot

MATERIALS
2 x 50 g balls dark brown DK
    (8-ply) wool
2 x 50 g balls beige DK
    (8-ply) wool
Oddments of DK (8-ply) wool in
    rust, cream, and light brown
1 pair 4 mm knitting needles
1 pair 3 mm knitting needles
Wool needle
Polyester fibre filling

Note The pleated fabric is created by pulling the yarn not in use tightly across on the wrong side. It is important to do this on each row. Carry the yarn on the back of the work and right across to the ends. It may seem a little slow to begin with but you will develop a rhythm.

Using 4 mm knitting needles and dark brown (A) DK (8 ply), cast on 98 sts. Work 8 rows garter st (every row knit). Join in beige (B).

Row 1: K1A, k6B, *k7A, k7B, rep from * to last 7 sts, k6A, k1B. As you knit, pull the yarn not in use very firmly behind, to draw up the pleats.

Row 2: K1B, k6A, *k7B, k6A, rep from * to last 7 sts, k6B, k1A. Keep yarn to the front in this row and continue to pull the yarn not in use tightly so that pleats remain firm.

These 2 rows form pattern. Continue in pattern until 48 rows have been worked.

Commence Decreases

Row 3: (rs) K2togA, k3B, k2togB, *k2togA, k3A, k2togB, k3B, k2togB, rep from * to last 7 sts, k2togA, k3A, k2togB.

Row 2: K1B, k4A, *k5B, k5A, rep from * to last 5 sts, k4B, k1A.

Row 3: K2togA, k1B, k2togB, *k2togA, k1A, k2togA, k2togB, k1B, k2togB rep from * to last 5 sts, k2togA, k1A, k2togB.

Row 4: K1B, k2A, *k3B, k3A, rep from * to last 3 sts, k2B, k1A.

Row 5: K2togA, k1B, *k2togA, k1A, k2togB, k1B, rep from * to last 3 sts, k2togA, k1B.

Row 6: K1B, k1A, *k2B, k2A, rep from * to last 2 sts, k1B, k1A.

Row 7: (K2togA) twice, *k2togB, k2togA, rep from * to last 4 sts, (k2togB) twice.
Break off yarn, thread through rem sts, pull up tightly and fasten off.
Make 2.

To Make Up Darn in any loose ends. With right sides facing, stitch the two halves together working from the centre top down each side for 5 cm. Tie off firmly. Join sides together at the bottom edge, stitching up each side for 3–4 cm. Turn right side out.

KNITTED BALLS

Using 3 mm knitting needles and one of the oddments of DK (8-ply) yarn, cast on 12 sts. Make 3 balls, each in a different oddment colour following the instructions for the Pomp and Circumstance tea cosy.

TWISTED CORDS

Using 3 mm knitting needles and DK (8-ply) wool, cast on 25 sts.

Row 1: Inc in every st (knit into front and back of each st).
Cast off purlwise.
Make 3, one in each oddment colour.

To Decorate Cosy Attach the 3 balls firmly to the top of the tea cosy and the 3 twisted cords inbetween.

Index